Muhammad Ali

by Wilfrid Sheed

a portrait in words and photographs

An Alskog Book
Thomas Y. Crowell Company

November 1974.

The first Patterson fight, Las Vegas, 1965.

An Alskog Book

Text copyright © 1975 by Wilfrid Sheed

Photographs copyright © 1975 by Neil Leifer

Jacket photograph copyright © 1975
by Curt Gunther, Camera 5

Photographs copyright © 1975
and previously copyrighted by: Y. Aono/Liason, Howard
Bingham, Black Star, Camera Five, Harry Coughanour, Frank
Dandridge, James Drake, Robert Halmi, C. Thomas Hardin,
Thomas Hopker, Fred Kaplan, Mark Kauffman, Neil Leifer,
Phil Leonian, Danny Lyon, Richard Meek, New York Times,
Photoreporters, Ted Polumbaum, Ken Regan, Lowell Riley,
Herb Scharfman, Lawrence Schiller, Flip Schulke, John
Shearer, Peter Angelo Simon, Sports Illustrated, Time-Life
Pictures, Transworld, Tony Triolo, United Press, World Wide
Photos, World Wide Press

Publisher: Lawrence Schiller
Design director: Will Hopkins
Text editor: Jay Acton
Copy editor: Judith R. Schiller
Editorial advisor: Sean Callahan
Editorial staff
    Text: Pat Underwood, Vince Trankina
    Photography: Maria Schuman, Sue Terry
Design assistant: Julie Asher Palladino
Production manager: Ira Fast

Color separation:
National Color Graphics, New York, New York

Typesetting:
Computer Typesetting Services, Glendale, California

Paper: Warren Paper Co.; Lindenmeyr Paper Merchants

Printing: R.R. Donnelley & Sons, Chicago, Illinois

Library of Congress Catalog Card Number: 75-18714
ISBN: 0-690-00958-5
First Printing

Published simultaneously in Canada
Printed in the United States of America

4

Ali with second wife Belinda in the Chicago bakery where they met.

Contents

The Cleveland Williams fight, November 1966, Houston, Texas.

*Ali in a postfight interview watching an
instant replay of his knockout over Liston.*

Prologue to a Heavyweight

Muhammad Ali believes he is the most famous man in the world, and he may be onto something (since Pope John, name another). His picture hangs in African mud huts, where they don't always even know what he does for a living; Arab kings lay villas on him like Kleenex: he is the toast of England and the fastest route to an argument in America, and altogether the noisiest piece of work since Telstar made possible the global shriek.

He claims to be everywhere, like oxygen (his critics say pollution). But whatever the chemical content, so much fame has to be important—if fame is important. Ali is a rallying point for Black Americans, and a link between them and the Third World. His persona, which began as a cheerful promotion stunt, has ballooned grotesquely into a political and religious symbol.

So far he has used this potential power mainly to promote himself and hustle his fights. But he has a long life ahead of him. His physician, Dr. Ferdie Pacheco, calls him a marvelous piece of machinery, capable of fighting five more years at least. But when this palls, as it must, there will be a mass of energy and charm and spare fame

on the loose, and things are going to rumble.

For better or worse. My object in this book will be to look for clues to this in his past and present, and to take a biopsy on his fame (some kinds, like Liberace's are absolutely non-negotiable at the power bank; others like the Beatles' can cause convulsions). Will the planet earth feel the good of his coming, or will only the black half of it? Or will we all live to curse our monster—or forget him?

We the public are the only thing crazier and more unpredictable than Ali, and in the coming years we will be his toughest opponent. My hunch, as I begin this book, is that the champ will not quit lightly, to the obscurity of his own bar and of sportswriters' memories. He has tasted stronger stuff, and he will do anything, even become a great man, a saint or a scoundrel to hang onto his fame: because fame was always what it was all about.

Even a genius must begin somewhere. The ultimate goal is pure fame, as undifferentiated and unqualified as God's—just a face, a signature, a name people murmur—but one must start as a famous some-

A young Cassius Clay in 1961 at Angelo Dundee's Fifth Street Gym in Miami.

thing: boxer, poet, loudmouth, whatever. (In this, as in all that follows, it must be emphasized that Ali does not necessarily sit around thinking, how can I be famous. It is a blind biologic groping for the limelight, awesome in its accuracy.)

The form Ali chose, that of heavyweight champion, has certain built-in advantages and disadvantages. Predecessors like Jack Dempsey, Gene Tunney, Joe Louis have all had a certain kind of fame, no more no less. The championship is like one of those frames you stick your head through to be photographed: the face is your own, but the clothes and posture belong to the management.

Within these limits, the world heavyweight champion occupies a guaranteed special position in the great celebrity freak-show. Although the sport of boxing appears to be sinking into the sea, he reigns on in splendid detachment, like the last Romanoff or the Aga Khan (what is an Aga anyway? Is it a place or something you do?). The Champ is a King without a country; and on the rare occasions he chooses to fight, his Sport lives again for one night, like a fairy-tale Kingdom.

And mind you, this is true of the meanest lunk who ever wore the belt; old ladies who don't know a hook from a jab are odds on to know his name; and old men dream dreams of John L. Sullivan clobbering him. Muhammad Ali did not so much invent this role as reinterpret and enlarge it, the way Moms Mabley might have reinterpreted the Royal Crown of England if it came her way.

Unlike other celebrities who can do as they damn please, the heavyweight champion has up to now had certain moral responsibilities, more like a spiritual leader. As the strongest man in the world, one on one, he is supposed to set an example in civility, like an English policeman. He is expected to be a good influence—much better say, than a middleweight—and to show kids how a potential killer disports himself off the field. He must also "wear his crown with honor" and above all, display that "indefinable something called class."

Now "class" is a fine thing if it just means not being Jimmy Connors and abiding by the decencies of one's sport. And it can be even better, if it means the perfect gesture of courage or generosity, which jocks make on average about as often as bankers. But, there is also an element of domestication about it too, as the beast is trained to use the right knife and fork and

16

to make gracious speeches at banquets, and it is this that the very concept of Ali challenged most directly. B.C. (before Clay, as opposed to Ali Domini), the symptoms of class included being lordly, inarticulate and unswervingly tasteful, in short, the perfect butler.

This may date back to the literal class origins of Sport when his lordship had to mix it with the villagers. When a gentleman played, or wagered on, an inferior, each agreed to become something in between —aloof, dignified, "sportsmanlike," and this requirement has hung over professional athletes ever since, from Joe DiMaggio to the titled jockeys of England; but especially over that Queen for a day, that Lord of the streets, the World Heavyweight Champion.

That is, until Ali, the tortured clown and laughing martyr on the jacket. Suddenly we had a champion who refused to sit still in his robes and make like an Archbishop. The outside world had changed, and this electronic baby was here to announce it—to the crustiest, most tradition-bound sport of them all. "I am the prettiest." Murder in the cathedral. Instead of honoring the title, he would use it to express *himself*—and in turn, he would re-invent the

title for us; he would dance it out and put it in rhyme, and then he would explode from it, a man in his own right.

He would even accomplish the one essential of supercelebrity, which no heavyweight since Tunney has even contemplated: he would be interesting to women. And not just to groupies, and not just sexually. The millions of women of all intelligences who support our fan magazines demand a wider range than that. The dream-lives of wives and mothers and other shut-ins are complex and subtle, and Ali proposes himself to them in several ways totally outside boxing—as son and father and free spirit, to name just a few. For a believer in the world's most male sexist religion, he has achieved an extraordinary female following from tots to older persons. If you throw in his standing as a religious and political figure to the black world, you may have the celebrity of celebrities, the all-time champion in this modern art form of simply being famous.

Some of the older sportswriters clucked like dowagers over the eruption of this jive-ass intruder who was no mere comic servant in the Archie Moore or Lee Trevino tradition, but a comic king. Specifically, they felt that his crazy boasting and theatrical tantrums were vulgarizing his sport to the level of wrestling. And although boxing might itself be seedy and gangster-ridden and down to its last cigar, it was still a repository of Class, like the racetrack or the Kennel Club. Ali's antics might be keeping the sport alive by main force but they didn't want it alive on those terms. Those old-timers with racial hangups were doubly tortured—Joe Louis had been a terrific butler, a veritable Jeeves—but I'll get to them later. For the more honorable of them, a white man like Joe Namath would have been just as bad.

It was just that a generation of vacant-eyed young punks seemed to be taking over everywhere—playing the camera instead of the sport, dropping their pants to fill the house, clawing, kicking and drooling over money. No class at all.

Ali has since been widely blamed for these creatures. Whenever a Bobby Fischer or an Ilie Nastase occurs, he is promptly christened the Muhammad Ali of chess or tennis or canyon-jumping. Princess Anne is the Ali of horseback riding, and there are several in literature. (I'm told that one of them has even turned up in indoor squash.) They are all variously praised for putting their sports on the map and blamed for reducing them to the level of wrestling—to which, in fact, most of public life has been reduced; and they were all inevitable the day the first picture tube was discovered. Even that *reductio ad absurdum*, Jimmy Connors, whose naturally bad manners are actually encouraged as box office by his manager, the last corruption of pedagogy, could have been predicted.

No doubt they, or their accountants, learned some of Ali's techniques, so his place in the history of bullshit is secure. Yet to some of us, he was always a puzzling exception, a blowhard we didn't mind. Some reasons for this were obvious enough. Although he foreshadowed this generation of hustling dudes—he is inevitably a creature of his times—he was startlingly unlike them in certain essentials. For one thing, he really seemed childlike, and not just a dwarfish mutation out of *Oliver Twist*. For another, he had horse-and-buggy values to reassure the older crowd. Once on Joe Namath's old talk show, he expressed his disapproval of his host's moral philosophy, and refused to kid about it—reducing Joe to the usual foolish giggles. He also refuses to do certain commercials and despises black exploitation films.

Then as he went along, he seemed to

19

invent a new kind of Class all his own. He uses the word dignity a lot, even between making faces at Howard Cosell, and we're just beginning to see what he means by it. He is indeed a creature of the tube and a master of it; he watches the news and he knows the names and how they're doing. "Twiggy and the Beats have come and gone and I'm still here." Like many new stars he thinks like a fan, and the fan tells him who he is and what to do. Yet, within that refracted world of film looking at film, he has improvised an Ethic, a sense of when and how to kid, and of how to protect his private self, that has added something new to the art of celebrityhood in general, and the art of the Negro Entertainer in particular. As a boxer he has brought gifts of menace and bluff that other superstars can only manage when they're drunk. He has exhausted the platonic possibilities of the heavyweight as celebrity.

At the same time, he was fuelling, and being fuelled by a plucky little industry that needed help—namely, sportswriting. Newspapers still grant rolling acreage to this specialty, even in an era when concerned readers have most likely seen the game already in infinite replay. So sportswriters have devised their own form of New Jour-nalism to fill the space, a mishmash of gossip, depth psychology, cooking hints; not to mention the wife's point of view, the children's point of view, and the old-daddy-still-plucking-buzzards-in-Maine's point of view. No profession has ever been more scrutinized; there *had* to be interesting athletes.

So imagine if you will, 50 of these tormented vultures from the Sports Department trying to scavenge a story from the grunts of the average heavyweight. What a blessing to find one who actually talked—never mind what he said. Ali was a godsend to reactionaries and reformers alike. Denouncing him took as many lines as praising him, and either way one's own point of view got a sumptuous airing.

The sportswriters needed him the way a crime reporter needs his rapist. Connors and Fischer were OK, but you could only shake your jowls at them once or twice. Ali was inexhaustible. When such a hole in the newspaper exists someone will eventually rise to fill it, but Ali rose so magnificently that non-sportswriters and kibitzers began to horn in on our beleaguered brothers, until the press room looked like Madame de Stael's salon in Paris.

Hence this book.

Ali through the Looking Glass

Why write about Ali? Why paint the Mona Lisa? Because he is pure subject: a Mona Lisa that talks—and becomes more mysterious with every word. Norman Mailer is awed by his ego; critics are stunned by his poetry. Even writers on economics and botany must be tempted to have a whack at him; the Everest of our profession. And, in fact, he has inspired more good writing (not just writing) than anyone in the current sports world.

My own writing has been mainly in and around the arts, with side trips into sports, so my interest is first of all in Ali the artwork—and in Ali the artist who created the artwork: where did he get the footwork and the mouth? What is he *for?* Deeper than that—is there a wizard behind the curtain, who gives off those booming sounds and giant-size reflections, or is Ali a collection of special effects, a talking and strutting machine with no one in charge? Celebrities in general are chosen, like the calendar of Saints, to meet certain needs: thus, Frank Sinatra is the patron celebrity of comebacks, Liza Minnelli of daughters,

Jackie Onassis of curious marriages. When no saint can be found, it may be necessary to invent one: hence St. Christopher, Jack Benny, Alice Cooper. What need does Ali service? He was a jester for the Camelot years and a suffering saint for Vietnam, but in each case he did it so eccentrically, and left such a wayward signature, that his real mission seemed to be simply to surprise us. We need Ali because we need puzzles (Howard Hughes is not enough). But is there someone else inside this super-salesman—a secret inviolable self? If so, what does it look like? Does it match his face or his antics, or is it quite different?

Visually speaking, Ali lives in a hall of mirrors, like the book you're looking at. At least two of his closest assistants are photographers, so every moment of his day is recorded, and "I am the prettiest" is verified over and over. Having stared myself into a near-trance at thousands of these pictures (and read myself into stupefaction with thousands of words) I can almost see him in the mirror when I shave, although I cut easily. So we'll start with the looking

25

glass Ali, the media creature, and then try to step through the glass and see if there's anything in back.

But before I do that, and disappear altogether, I should like to digress like Victor Borge and tell you why I am here tonight, and what happened on the way over.

My first encounter with boxing was unpromising; me and another six-year-old, eyes shut tight, blasting away with bloated gloves like a pillow-fight gone mad. I remember dancing lights (probably a 50-watt bulb, but it seemed like the Garden) and a sense that my eyelashes had been broken one by one. Pandemonium. I formed an immediate resentment at being punched in the nose which has never left me and which comes back vicariously when I see Ali sacrificing his midriff, taking punishment beyond belief to spare his pretty face; and conversely, hunting the other man's head, breaking the first commandment of boxing that you work your way up by destroying his stomach, his supply lines—and going instead for the seat of his vanity and embarrassment: his face.

Later I learned to jab accurately enough, though without force. The memory of that first fist going off like a bedspring in my lower forehead caused me to bring the hand back too fast, uncommitted. Ali is a defensive fighter, and I took this right off for a mark of imagination. "See? No marks, no cuts. Pretty as ever." Clearly my kind of fighter.

I quit the game in no time, when I saw a classmate rattle the small bag like a stenographer and I imagined my head dangling from the chain. But I retain the tingle of a memory, touched with wonder concerning this primeval sport which is played without balls or bats or goal-lines

or bases or other draperies, like a chess game played with naked brain waves: just two men parrying, probing, asserting, with their hands; two conversationalists, witty or saturnine—Ali making a jest with his left that Frazier doesn't see, Frazier countering with a gut-joke of his own, courtesy of the boys—two men writing new scripts every night beyond their own comprehension.

Ali, of course, is the master scriptwriter, the comprehender, the artist. But in no other sport could he do this so well, tattoo his name on his work (Frazier's face only needed a signature) while leaving his own palette blank; and significantly, no other sport appeals to him. The Clays are an artistic family, and boxing is the next best thing.

Or is this too fancy a picture by half? Writers who enjoy boxing are notorious comic figures, like lecherous clergymen or honest politicians, and they are never deemed funnier than when they are making lofty aesthetic claims for the sport. So let me impose another black and white picture on this: not of two artists but of two old craftsmen frantically tailoring their shop-worn styles to fit each other's, taking in the jab a little, letting out the hook. This is the reality of boxing much of the time, and it is this often enough that stirs the drab soul of the novelist. Not machismo, God knows, at that level, but the small tricks of survival.

Ali seems to be a rare exception. Yet could it be that even he is sometimes reduced to this world of the frantically drawn diagram, and the search for fractional advantages? And that what we take for art is often an extraneous flourish, a gesture that has nothing to do with boxing? Watch him with both pictures in mind. The mad

28

artist, the plodding pro.

Anyway, I felt that his technique matched mine tolerably well when he came along, even to keeping his hands low (a trick I picked up from Jack Dempsey). Inside every sports fan is the kid who first got hooked, and the boxing fan in me is no more than 11 years old, hitching at his drawers with one mitten and thumbing his nose with the other. We wrote this book in collaboration. The older partner likes Ali for another reason. He picked up some change on the first Liston fight, and more along the way (we'll forget about Foreman—Ali was talking funny before that one) and you have to admire anyone who does that for you.

One other personal note, and that concerns the race question. I believe every other kid in my school rooted for Billy Conn to beat Joe Louis—not that it was a particularly red-neck school, but because there were a lot of pint-sized professional Irishmen calling the tune in these matters. Yet the unanimity puzzled me. Louis was by way of being widely respected, the very model of a champión, who had served his country by destroying Max Schmeling. Yet it went without saying you were for Conn.

I was no prodigy of enlightenment myself—just too dumb to know there was a race problem. In my first nine years in England, the only blacks I knew of were princes in robes, who checked into the Seat of Empire from time to time, and Paul Robeson, whose records we played to rags. When we got to America in 1940, I became an ardent Joe Louis fan, without complications. From some old copies of the newspaper *PM*, I see that he was fighting Arturo Godoy (second time) the week we landed, and it must have made a good impression.

A beautiful fighter, the only one in my opinion who could have hacked it with Ali at his best (his worst is another story), and I would have admired him anyway. But the sullen unenthusiasm of my friends drove me to extremes of adulation for this sphinx-like fellow, who spoke only once a year, but each time, a pearl. "He can run but he can't hide" for this very Conn fight. "No one got hurt but the customers," for the first Walcott.

People have since contrasted Louis the gentlemen with Ali the guttersnipe, and Joe's apparent feats of Uncle-Tomism in World War II do seem to clash with Ali's stubborn resistance to the Vietnamese mess. Yet one always sensed a truculence, possibly even a contempt beneath Louis' good manners; his silence said the same thing as Ali's mouth. Don't touch me. I'll play for you if the price is right, but don't touch me. Louis was his own man in everything he said and did. (Besides which, that was a very different war, and a different era.)

Continuing my racial training—at 15, I went over and over to see Ali's hero Jack Johnson demolishing Stanley Ketchel in Nat Fleischer's classic movie, *Kings of the Ring*. Ketchel had nettled the great man by knocking him down or causing him to slip, and Johnson had bounded across the ring so fast his middleweight opponent couldn't move. Such speed in a heavy was unbeatable—or so I thought. "Dempsey would have killed him," said my ring-wise friends. "Him *and* Louis." It wasn't that I especially liked black fighters; it was that nobody else liked them at all, and I was driven to it by sheer cantankerousness. So, I became Johnson's leading *post facto* 15-year-old fan if anybody gave a damn.

Looking further into Johnson, I found

something else interesting: that he was the patron boxer of outsiders like me; in fact, foreigners actually used him *against* America, as they would later use Ali. When I got to my father's hometown of Sydney, Australia, I found that every old man there claimed to have been in the front row when Johnson knocked out Tommy Burns in 1908 to become the first black champion, and everyone of them had bet Johnson. It was one of the two or three events of the century down there, and older Australian fight fans still bear a superstitious reverence for "Little Arthur," as he was called. "Although he wouldn't fight Sam Langford," one of them told me gravely, that was his one weakness. "He was afraid of the Boston tar-baby."

If one is placing Ali in the history of black fighters, this remark is significant. Sam Langford was the first or second most brilliant black fighter of his day (we'll never know) but no promoter thought it worth his time to put two blacks in the ring together: any snaggle-toothed white hope was a better draw. Johnson would have had to fight Langford in an alley, which he wisely declined to do. Compared with other American sports, boxing may seem like a miracle of tolerance, but the ghost of racism still hangs around the gym: only now, we convert one of the two black boys to white, and root for him. At least Ali seems to see it that way, and taunts us with it: I ain't going to be the white boy. Let *him* be the white boy tonight.

Jack Johnson taught Ali how to rub our noses in our own racism, and Ali acknowledges the debt (even an original has influences); in fact, he identified totally with Johnson when he saw the play *Great White Hope*. Yet were they really so alike?

And do people really hate Ali because he is black? At times he almost seems to be forcing us to make racism the issue. Johnson at least had no such problem. My father saw him box an exhibition in a Sydney vaudeville house and somebody from Burns' camp casually shouted up "yeller streak." By the time my father looked back, Johnson's opponent was already on his back. This cry, and much worse ones, followed the champ everywhere.

In those days anyone felt free to call a nigger anything: we hadn't even learned hypocrisy. And it was imperative to find some flaw of mind or heart in the black champion. When Johnson taunted his opponents ("see my yellow streak, Mr. Tommy?") he was not just doing commercials; he was teaching the Man a running lesson in manners and biology. And since blacks in those days were known to have no character, no stamina, no guts or intelligence, he had a lot to teach. But surely those lessons had been learned by Ali's time?

To some extent, Ali replayed Johnson's career as farce. The last thing I read about Jack was in the *New Yorker* "Talk of the Town" section; it seems the old boy, still in crackling command of his faculties, had been spotted at a flea circus, where the claim was that he had the thickest skull in the world—thick as a buffalo. (So much for heavyweights who set *bad* examples.) Nothing like that will happen to Ali. He probably won't even wind up as broke as Joe Louis. Celebrities perform over a net these days, fame alone being so lucrative, so that even their most gallant gestures are suspect.

Yet when Ali refused to step forward to be inducted into the Vietnam massacre, he and many others believed that he was treated significantly worse than a white man would have been, indicating that Johnson's world is still out there, however slickly disguised. It has changed, of course, just as Ali is a much more streamlined character than Johnson was. He is nothing like as "bad" or sinister as that old reprobate, who affronted Whitey by romancing his women (Ali has scrupulously avoided being a sexual threat so far), and Ali's irony seems more playful—or perhaps we read black irony better now. Johnson was caught and eventually jailed on a trumped-up Mann Act charge which summarized white fear and revulsion; Ali's case was eventually dismissed. Johnson was a nightmare, Ali more of an irritation.

And yet the desire to shut that mouth somehow—or failing that to silence his fists, to get him out of sight—must have been almost as strong. To some extent it was Ali's doing (he'd already made a fortune out of annoying people) but not entirely. Because if blackness wasn't as bad a crime as it had been, Youth was worse, and Ali was a horrible example of that, too, with his arrogance and his unisex cry "I am the prettiest." So the old men ganged up on him and for three years and a bit, he couldn't get a fight on the mainland, even on an Indian reservation (where they said "he would desecrate the land our brave boys have walked on") and he could not get a passport to fight abroad. He was not as lonely as Johnson was. He had a booming noise machine called Black Power, and a squeaky one called liberal opinion in his corner. But they weren't enough to keep the hate out—the pickets and the crazy letters. Technology has concentrated our attention, and improved the transmission of hate, as well as love, and Ali must have

received at least as much as Johnson did—to go with his two suitcases of favorable Muslim mail.

Remember, I'm still working from the outside. And it was almost as hard to tell how much Ali was really suffering as it is with his fellow Capricorn Nixon. (I don't believe in Astrology, but Capricorns are conceived around income tax time, and tend to be shifty.) Ali seemed a bit more serious, but he kept right on posturing through his troubles and it was hard to take

Jack Johnson, 1908.

31

(preceding page) On the road in 1963.
(right) As light heavyweight gold medalist
at the Rome Olympics, 1960.

him altogether seriously as a martyr. We signed things for him, but we signed all kinds of things in those days—it was hard to take *us* seriously in fact. Ali had heard about this cat Johnson, and was doing a hip rendition for the sixties; and we, connoisseurs of non-events, wept crocodile tears and did the black handshake.

I had mixed feelings about Ali, which is entirely correct. He still comes to us as a media creation, geared to canned laughter and tears. Yet two things persuaded me that the face in the mirror was sincere when he refused induction and had his title ripped off him. One was his religion, and we'll get to that later; I'll just say for now that his decision cost him money. And since the only certain way I know to judge spiritual leaders is the size of their bankbooks (and that goes from the Maharishi of Moolah on up to Dorothy Day with her indestructible shopping bags), Ali impressed me as the real thing.

The second convincer was something that happened to me as a kid, which will round off the personal memoir side of this and fling me back into the faceless public.

Back in the middle forties, we had a black doorman at our building whose name was George and who had the best manners this side of heaven. I guess you'd call him a Tom now, but those manners would have looked good on anyone: unobtrusive, evenhanded (you didn't have to be white), unfailingly alert—real class, as described above, and then some.

Anyway, it was George's pleasure to take in the fights at the Garden (which is why he comes to mind now) and he used to take me along occasionally; and I remember particularly watching Rocky Graziano plodding around the ring with his

right fist cocked, showing the full range of his technique, in pursuit of a stumblebum called Harold Green. In memory—and this cannot be literally true—he only threw the punch once, and that was that. KO in the third round.

However, back to George. One summer's day, we were squatting on the doorsteps fanning ourselves and shooting the breeze ("rapping" was unknown at the time) and I said, in reference to the baseball team, "I guess you hate the Yankees." It was a hot day, even George was sweating a little, and he apparently mistook my meaning. "Yes, I hate the Yankees," he said, in a suddenly murderous voice. "You're damn right I hate the Yankees." And he launched into an attack on the white man, North and South, such as I have never heard before or since—enough to make Eldridge Cleaver sound like a pussycat and Ali a member of the Klan. There was nothing personal about it. He talked as one friend to another. The white man was simply the worst abomination in history, and we both deplored abominations did we not? When he was done, he became again the perfect English gentleman, smiling at the white tenants who came and went in the heat, and no more was said.

I'm not sure, but I believe that George was among the doormen who protested when we had an interracial meeting in our apartment: so many Negroes would ruin the building's reputation, they felt.

Maybe everybody has a George, and a baptism in race warfare. Anyway, I believed Ali was sincere.

Back now in the crowd that follows Ali everywhere—that *is* Ali—I am just another white face. As such, we spot him first in Rome at the 1960 Olympics prancing

34

down the Via Veneto with his arm through a surprised Bing Crosby's. He is already a hustler, and has been since the age of 12 when he knocked on neighbors' doors in Louisville to tell them about his fights on a local TV show. But it is still unfocussed hustle—hustle for its own sweet sake. *Newsweek* calls him "an amiable, unsophisticated young man who loves life and people and success and fame." He rebuts a Marxist heckler by telling him that people don't get bitten by alligators in the U.S.—an early glimpse into his awesome thought processes. But the trademarks, the poems and prophecies, will come later: and these are learned behavior. All he began with was a blind desire to *be* somebody—and enjoy himself while doing it.

In those days, he was still nine parts boxing to one part mouth—and the boxing was something to behold. His technique at 16 and 17 in the Golden Gloves was of a sophistication unknown in that hairy shambles of an event. He could already hook off the jab, which is beyond some professionals, and he had mastered his great gift of depth perception—judging the length of his opponent's arms and bobbing an inch or so out of range. In one match with a burly Army champion, he fell to his nemesis, a left hook, but he was up in no time, poised as ever (most kids go completely to pieces and wander off in the wrong direction) and ready to kill. His opponent's legs were still twitching minutes later.

It is sometimes forgotten that, like many great entertainers, Ali had put in a full career before we'd heard of him. He'd had over 100 amateur fights (which might account for his head-hunting: body punches counting for less in a short bout) and his defects were by then as ingrained as his

virtues. Eddie Futch, the trainer, who has had a hand in both of Ali's professional defeats (Norton and Frazier), says Ali had so much natural ability that he never learned some of the fundamentals: he could always outrun his mistakes.

His technical shortcomings actually served to make him more exciting and salable, by adding a cliff-hanging or Perils of Pauline quality to his work. At Rome, the experts immediately spotted not one but two fatal flaws. Ali sometimes keeps his hands too low to protect his face properly, and he pulls his head back from punches, which could get him killed by a follow-up. Futch noticed a third: he always moved clockwise.

To be fair to the experts, these really are fatal flaws. Many young fighters have come to grief imitating Ali—in fact he may be the worst influence since Ernest Hemingway. But his speed and judgment always allowed him to escape by a whisker. "Defense ain't the hands, it's the legs," he says, and by dancing so precisely out of range, he can actually fight like the Venus de Milo, without any arms at all. Then, like a parent playing with a child, he can offer his face to be hit, only to snap it back, until the child collapses with frustration. Thus, Ali v. Foreman.

Anyway, at the Rome Olympics, he was felt to be promising, but not as promising as Floyd Patterson had been in 1956. As soon as he cleans up those flaws, we'll see. Then when he turned pro and began moving up in class, with triumph after triumph, the warnings continued, more ominous than ever. A minor fighter called Ernie Banks dropped him on his drawers with a left. Then Futch came in with a boy called Charlie Powell who made appoint-

(preceding page) His original backers,
the Louisville Group, 1963.
(right) Liston can't answer the bell in the first fight, Miami.

ments with Ali's clockwise rotation and rocked him for two rounds before missing an appointment himself. Vulnerability was part of the package, and it was given a lifetime lease by one Doug Jones, who not only hit him over the low hands and with the head back but lived to tell the tale.

A couple of other things showed in the Jones affair. One was that Jones, a journeyman whose sole mission in life seems to have been to fight this fight and demonstrate this one point, stumbled into the best way to fight Ali, which is simply to dull him down. Jones positively refused to dance with him, but stood stolidly in the middle of the ring waiting for something to happen, and fighting in flurries. Ali responded well enough to win—I only said that Jones' way was the best way, not that it would succeed—but he couldn't fight his classic fight, and sometimes he gets angry and bored when this happens, and he fights like a stuffed panda.

The other thing the Jones fight demonstrated was that the propaganda machine had already gotten in its deadly work and no one was quite rational about Ali. His famous practice of predicting which round his opponent would fall in had taken on a certain sacred impressiveness with the assistance of the 2,000-year-old Archie Moore in his last fight. Moore had waddled around the ring at Ali's pleasure, collapsing on cue. So the prophetic mumbo-jumbo became briefly believable, perhaps even to Ali himself. In Jones' case, he said he would win in four and when he didn't, it was like the death of God. People rapidly assumed that he was a total fraud, and they booed when he won a unanimous verdict.

Reviewing the fight films now, it is clear that Ali fought a most satisfactory fight that night, adapting himself to his loss of divinity and falling back on layers of professionalism. The fourth round itself was terrible—Ali was so eager to make his prophecy come true that he swung with his arms instead of his body, like a beginner—and the fifth round was rueful and melancholy, as he came to terms with mortality. But the rest was crisp as lettuce.

Anyhow, the scribes and pharisees now sought ways to put him down. They brought up the fatal flaws again and again. They said he lacked a single knockout punch, that freak of nature, as if a hundred knockout suggesters wasn't good enough. "He jabs you so sweet and cool," said Willie Pastrano—sort of like death from drowning. But he's obviously never jabbed the critics. And they said he couldn't take a punch himself—a myth as farfetched as Jack Johnson's yellow streak. There *had* to be something wrong with such an obnoxious fellow.

Once a prejudice gets rolling, there's no stopping it. Sonny Liston, his next port of call, was the most awesome thing in boxing at the time. He had twice demolished the ever-promising Floyd Patterson in something under six minutes all told, and he was good and ready for Clay. Even if the famous pre-fight needling was 90% promo, pretend emotions can become real ones with a dark spirit like Liston's, and he trained like a Stakhanovite for this fight. Yet no sooner had Clay beaten him than he became a washed-out bum. His physical condition worsened retroactively—he hadn't really trained at all. He was over 50, with grown-up grandchildren serving time. Besides which, he had thrown the fight.

A pattern had set in of downgrading Clay by belittling his opponents after the fact. Again, upon viewing the Liston films,

40

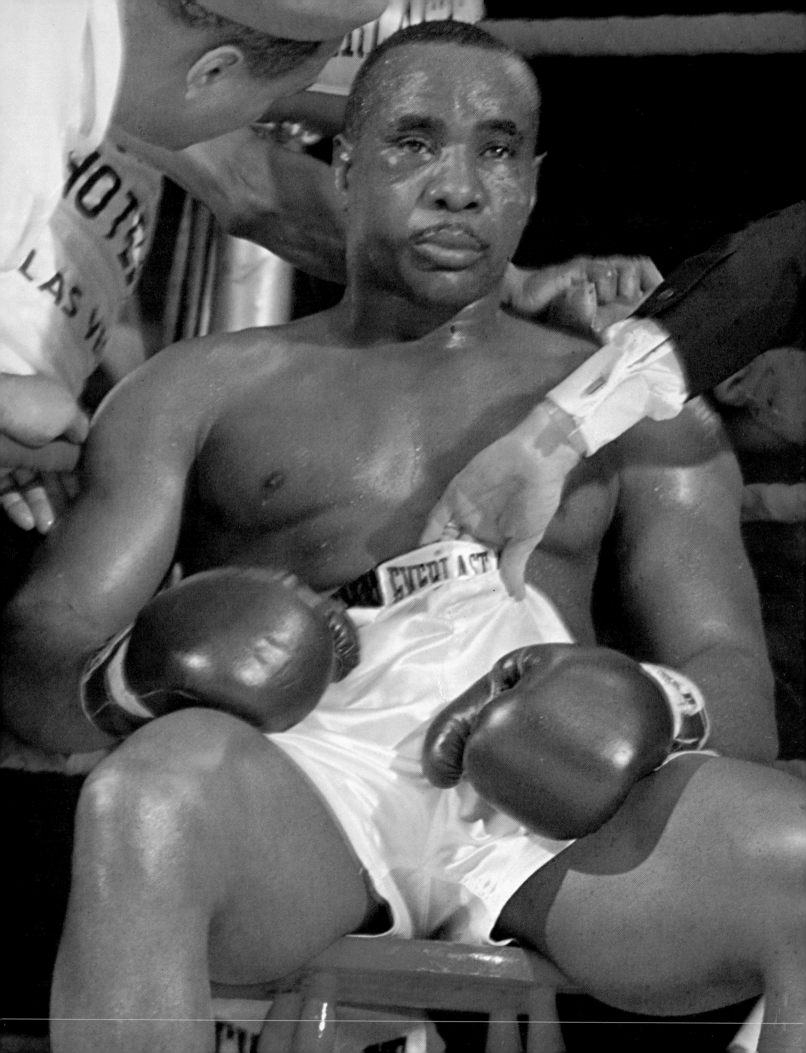

this becomes incredible. The first two, three rounds are among the most beautiful ever fought by the big men, with Liston prowling and charging at jungle speed, and Clay dancing clockwise away from the deadly left hook, but reversing himself just often enough for the hook to whistle past the other ear. He pulled his head back and he didn't get killed. He fought the fifth round half-blind from some caustic in his eye, but Sonny was exhausted by then from the fastest pace ever set in a heavyweight fight and Clay held him off like a matador, sticking and jabbing blindly and defending himself by braille.

Liston characteristically managed to leave a dark stain on ring history and on Clay's reputation. He didn't come out for the eighth round because of torn muscles in his arm—quite genuine as it turned out, but such is Sonny's aura that no one in the world believed him. Then, in the return match he managed a fainting spell in the first round, which again may have been genuine (microscopes later turned up an actual punch), but when referee Joe Walcott blew the count and gave him all evening to get up, Liston's rendition of a coma wouldn't have fooled a possum. He said he was afraid Ali would hit him again on the way up.

So Clay, by now Ali, was again short-changed by the critics, and might reasonably have become bitter about it. Yet, oddly enough, Ali the publicity machine that was growing alongside Ali the boxing artist, seemed to relish it. In his role of public enemy, it suited him to be under-rated. It meant that he could draw crowds even with the dogs of his division—which was going to be more and more necessary (the heavyweight division is chronically crawling with

42

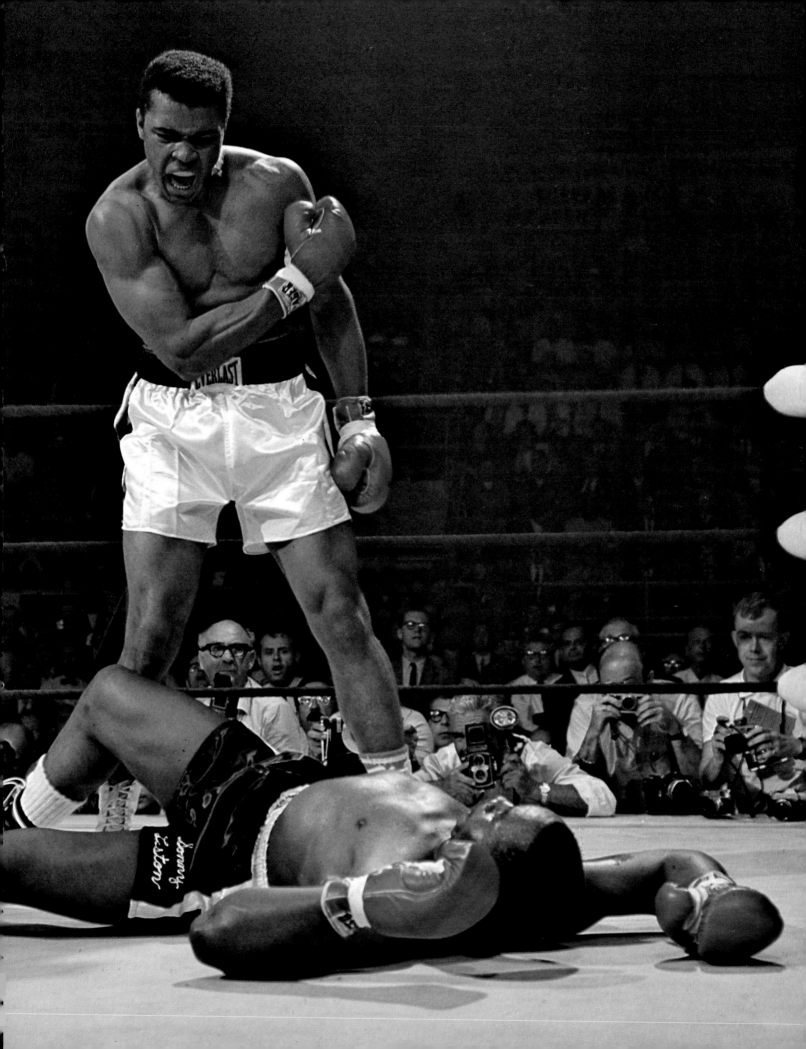

dogs). Clay would even challenge himself, come in overweight, change his style, anything to fill the house. Against George Chuvalo, he even tried standing still. His famous shuffle, which he had used as early as the Olympics (a crazy little war-dance, more suitable to entering an end zone) became more prominent. I used to suppose he only did it when his opponent was too weak to interrupt—again like a matador, when he kneels in front of his bull—but I find that he did it against Cleveland Williams in the second round when Williams was still zinging them in at top speed. (Williams was, it goes without saying, over the hill, a bullet riddled ex-con, but he looked awfully good that night.)

I have intentionally separated Ali the boxer from Ali the media freak, because a) the freak has only the most glancing relation with boxing—it is his occasion, his launching pad, but I'm convinced Ali would have found some other way to be famous and, b) because the freak has too often obscured the fighter and even held him up to ridicule. In this sense he has debased himself like a black entertainer after all—or like Jack Johnson. Ali is quite possibly the greatest fighter who ever lived, but many whites won't admit it under torture because of his Mouth. Instead, and to prove they are not bigoted, they have promoted Joe Louis, the good nigger, to this spot. Thus does Ali help his brothers.

After disposing of such worthies as Ernie Terrell and Williams and Zora Folley (who fought him the Jones way, and made a nice dignified showing before going down in seven), Ali's critics had to concede some merit in the chap. A fighter can only fight what's there, but this was not at all a bad crop by division standards. Jack Johnson's opponents were a scrawny bunch (Tommy Burns weighed 175 pounds), and Joe Louis was reduced to forming a Bum-of-the-Month Club.

In fact, the critics were down to their last trick. They said that Ali was all speed; that once that went, he would have nothing left. One thing you have to say for critics: they have endurance. Ali left the ring in celebrated circumstances that we'll get to in a moment and he lost some of his speed, and a new crop of heavyweights came along led by one Joe Frazier, an authentic star of the kind that dominates eras, and Ali came back on rubber legs and became champion again. And still there were critics—you can recognize them on sight—mumbling like spaced-out old boxers. No knockout punch. Foreman was out of shape. Marciano would have licked him. Yah.

Let us leave them to it. Ali's comeback was not only an astounding exhibition of character, it also proved as conclusively as anything can be proved in the impressionistic world of boxing, that he is indeed the greatest, even if he does say so himself. Older people were raised to believe that braggarts are always bluffing, but the new breed has no trouble believing. As the late Leonard Shecter remarked, "he had the kind of body that was revolutionizing football"—and he might have added track and swimming and tennis. That is, he was a big man with the speed and reflexes of a small one. Films indicate that his jabs are one-third faster than Sugar Ray Robinson, the great middleweight's, were—so he is not just fast for a big man, he is fast for a midget. What seemed like over-confidence was simply a judicious assessment by a very knowing professional. And don't be fooled

48

about that. He is, for all his flighty image, a meticulous student of old fight films and of the game in general. He learned to jab better from Willie Pastrano and to move side to side from Louis Rodriguez and to lay on the ropes from Sugar Ray against Jake La Motta in 1952.

Beyond his studies though, Ali simply thought and moved so much faster than his opponent that he always had time in hand, like Ted Williams in baseball. He spent the extra time promoting his business: shuffling, talking, relating to the crowd. He also used it to psych his opponents—since once you have a fighter thinking, the battle is half over. But the real marvel was that he had the time and the spare strength to do this stuff at all, against highly trained sharpshooters who can hit you between blinks. Again Ali the clown eclipses Ali the super-athlete.

When he came back, all the talk was about his legs. Gone for sure, said Joe Louis, the voice of God. And they certainly had slowed down some. He fought flat-footed now like a normal human. Against Jerry Quarry and Oscar Bonavena, the kind of pugs who are always around and who could be extras in a John Garfield movie, he was good enough, but the bounce was gone. Perhaps the legend of his speed had grown in his absence, even beyond the reality—he never danced more than a few rounds, or needed to—but the legs lacked enthusiasm now: they just carried him around, like an old station wagon.

Time now for the rendezvous with the new boy in town. Joe Frazier had taken over Dodge City and Tombstone and he wasn't the kind of man you want to meet on rubber legs. His fists went off like cannons, exploding through the TV set like

Sonny Liston's—especially the left, Ali's weakness. His legs were like tree trunks, and if you allowed him to plant them, they were a source of biblical strength. He was something of a trolley track fighter, who might have had trouble with Ali's old lateral speed, but to make up for this he had an irresistible forward charge that no number of punches could discourage. If oldtimers wanted to know how Ali would have done against Marciano, here was their answer: Frazier had the same bull-like qualities, the same courage, stamina and armor-plating, plus, in my opinion, a better punch and a smarter brain.

It is an odd law of physics that there can never be two great heavyweights at the same time: one rises as the other declines. The smallest edge in sharpness is multiplied infinitely in Big Man fighting; the slightly better man becomes the totally better man when such artillery is used. Hence the first Ali-Frazier fight was something of a suspension of natural law, as befits one beloved of Allah. There were two great heavyweights that night, and it was that mythical event—the Fight of the Century—as improbable a happening as the Great American Novel.

But before considering these later fights, which make a golden postscript like the Glorious Hundred Days of Napoleon between Elba and Waterloo, let's see how the publicity freak is doing, from gawky beginnings to his current purring efficiency, from carnival sideshow to celebrity champion material. Something happened to Ali before and during his exile that lifts these last fights out of ring history and into social history: he had become a symbol of a rather complicated sort, so that even your deaf grandmother had opinions about him.

Eggheads, or whatever you prefer to call us misfits who like sports for the wrong reasons, were drawn to Ali from the very beginning, although it is unlikely we have one opinion in common with him. Truly interesting superstars are hard to come by—their interestingness being absorbed so thoroughly into their art—and in a pinch, we have to make them interesting by sheer willpower. A gaseous bore like Casey Stengel, or a Chamber of Commerce humorist like Dizzy Dean becomes magically an American original (or so I am told by an outside observer who came to them cold; I have long since happily swallowed the myths myself).

So if an athlete actually *is* interesting, egghead excitement knows no bounds. To some extent Ali had to be invented too. A man whose idea of joke is to dress up in a sheet and say "boo" to his trainer is not that far above the run of jocks. So the early Ali is something of an artifact. He recites a poem while doing sit-ups, and the great A. J. Leibling says he bets T. S. Eliot couldn't do that—and we think *Ali* has said something funny. Ali I, or rather Cassius Clay, from the Olympics to Liston is a routine case of the making of a sports eccentric; with Cassius and his People concocting bits of business and the writers doing the rest.

In fact, young Cassius, like a new breed politician, even supplied his own gag writers. His famous signature line, "float like a butterfly, sting like a bee," came from Drew "Bundini" Brown—a legendary cutup who appears and disappears in Ali's life, like Sporting Life in *Porgy and Bess.* Ali's manager, Angelo Dundee, doubles as an inspired P.R. man, and may or may not have helped out with the poetry (he claims it was his idea in the first place). Let's say

that Ali is not above borrowing. In fact, he even lifted his pre-fight boasting from Georgeous George, the white wrestler.

Like all such synthetics, the early Cassius Clay was a slightly unsatisfactory figure. George Plimpton noted that his face did not always seem to match his material—whether he was raging or joking. Indeed, as with Bob Hope and President Ford and other wit-dispensers, there was some question whether he had any sense of humor at all. If Dundee and Bundini had been replaced by Billy Graham and Rod McKuen we might have had a whole different Clay.

He was still a natural force, featureless as the wind, irresistible if you like that kind of thing, but quite pointless. His first recorded interviews are poised and only the slightest bit sassy. Then he discovers, like Bernard Shaw, the humor of boasting. Then the poetry. Then some drawings for *Esquire.* It is like a salesman with a new line every year, and no need for a personality. Then seriousness (or is this a new line too?) hits him in mid-caper. The Vietnam War, the Black Muslim religion, marriage and children: these mixed into the old publicity-machine produced the unique ambiguities of Muhammad Ali, a man different enough from the early Clay to justify the change of name, the rebirth of a salesman as prophet.

Yet such a creation cannot be made out of nothing: so one looks again at the early Clay for clues. If his face was not quite right for humor or rage, it was certainly right for something: either something he hadn't found, or something he was hiding, or both.

Outside of his wildly original ring style, which told one plenty, there was always a faint touch of the poet—though it seldom came out in his poems. When he talked of his future, it was always in sensuous terms: a cool drive in a tomato-red Cadillac with the right fox, through a twilight city; a mansion on the hill with the decor lovingly described.

By now, we are used to athletes draped in fur and tiger skin: yet it is somehow always grosser and more pushy than Ali's early dreams. In contrast, even an elegant like Walt Frazier comes across as a vulgar robber baron. One sensed in Ali the artist's curse: that he would rather imagine his mansion than live in it; that if he lived in it, he would be bored, and would start imagining a different mansion—or a hovel, where the smell of food cooking would be sweeter than perfume. Every account of Ali begins with his restlessness, he paces, shadow-boxes, decides to leave town. Something great is always about to happen. But he is bored right now (unless he's watching a John Wayne movie). Out of this boredom and restlessness, artists traditionally feel obliged to make new realities and then more new realities.

Hence Ali, the myth-maker. "I must live my own legend," he says, but first he must invent it. He has invented a couple of pasts but this does not really grab him because, in the interests of divinity, it is better to have no past at all, so one can create oneself completely. Great prophets traditionally come from nowhere, and Ali does the next best thing, by vague flat answers to prying questions. His material is the formless future, on which he can impose infinite patterns. He daydreams for fun and he daydreams for exercise, and then he acts out his dreams comically, seriously, every way he knows how. In all of which, he

resembles a writer like Byron or a painter like Dali, more than any jock in easy memory. He has passed from sports-page eccentric to the real thing: even down to using a pen name.

In his first P.R. version of his origins, young Cassius Clay came off as a mean, rock-throwing kid running with the "baddest gangs" in Louisville. But this didn't sound right. His parents may or may not have been grindingly poor (versions differ on that too, from day to day like alternate side parking) but Clay was no street urchin. In repose, there is almost something of the rich kid in him, if not the downright aristocrat—which he might not bother to deny. So one is not surprised to learn from Jack Olsen's definitive book on the subject that the Clays are in fact a classy family, in whatever sense, with artistic interests, particularly on the graphic side.

His father is a sign painter, whose work is scattered through Louisville, but also a prolific amateur painter, with a studio designed like one of Ali's futuristic dreams. So that's where the decor comes from. Cassius, Sr. never quite made it, and quite reasonably, worked off his frustrations with an occasional jug, which turned him into a wild man. He was hauled into court several times for beating his wife, but never charged, because among other things, he had "street charm": outside the house and sober, you never met a nicer man. But if this at times tipped over into deference, he made it up at home by ripping up the white man and his works—planting seeds alternately of racism and accommodation.

I am told by those who know that being beaten up by a gifted father has a peculiar horror to it; all that intelligence coming at you, twisted and roaring. (I believe I've heard the sound from the next apartment, and it's like a cry from Hell.) Whether Ali's childhood was like this, or anything like this, it would be impertinent to guess—and he isn't saying. But Patrolman Joe Martin, who taught him to box at age 12, is quoted as reporting that he was obviously "scared to death of his father," which suggests at least that the old man was *unpredictable;* you had to guess his moods, read his face, know when to duck.

His mother, Odessa Grady Clay, is by all accounts as sweet as the wives of frustrated artists have to be, and Ali was and is very much attached to her. Again, this sounds more like the childhood of an artist than an athlete. There is a sweetness about Ali too, which he probably learned from his mama and which he cannot conceal behind the most ferocious grimaces; in all the pictures I've looked at, there is not one really nasty one. When Liston called him a fag, he was saying what any barfly would say to any poet—"you're not one of us"; he was referring to an openness to the feminine that every artist has—that Cassius, Sr. probably has, and which even a Liston might have if he'd let himself. When Ali kids with Bundini Brown, and even slaps him, there is a coquettishness about it that a lesser man would try to hide, even from himself.

Liston got what he deserved. Calling Ali a fag is not a recommended practice. After a shy and coltish start with girls, he has apparently played masterful catch-up ball. But he remains a gentle fellow by the standards of his calling, who genuinely loves children (and doesn't just Danny Kaye it) and who has peaceful dreams right before a fight. He also does, I'm told, a very funny fag imitation.

So the street gangs have to go. Young Ali seems, on the contrary, to have positively disliked random violence; he was often chased by bigger kids, and like boys who stammer or have funny names, he may have taken up boxing to calm his fears. At some unspecified point in his teens, he seems to have also discovered the pre-fight tantrum, that measured burst of hysteria, which shifts the balance of fear to his opponent. Whether he was really frightened or whether he lucked into it, it worked. Even a lumpish man like Liston was afraid he might be fighting a crazy man, so you can imagine what it did to the kids in Louisville.

By now, the tantrums are presumably automatic and have lost any base they

might have had in fear. Yet it is interesting that he still has the worst ones with the fighters he has most reason to fear (Liston and Frazier) and can barely summon a sneer for a patty-cake like Henry Cooper; and interesting that the tantrums are physiologically sincere—his blood pressure and pulse go crazy, so much so that after his masterpiece of tantrums before the first Liston fight, there was some question whether he was fit to go on.

Whether or not Ali ever did have the yellow streak of which his hero Jack Johnson had been accused, it has not hurt his intellectual appeal. Eggheads love to see signs of fear in athletes—it makes them one of us. Small reporters are especially prone to ask about it. "Were you afraid, huh, huh?" In Ali's case, it would also put him in the great American tradition of Teddy

Roosevelt and Hemingway, the sissy who made a man of himself, keeping vestigial links with the other sissies and giving them hope.

From external evidence, on the wrong side of the mirror, I doubt that there's much to it though. Ali himself says it is not fear but emotional depression that he feels—a mutation of fear or stage fright which he exorcises by hi-jinks; but fundamentally Ali's gland of publicity has so outgrown other childish emotions that even fear is its servant. One notes that he is more likely to blow up at blacks than whites, which suggests a nagging respectfulness after all; but it also suggests that he prefers to work with actors he trusts, and who will play the scenes right. Frazier, it may be forgotten, led a lamentable rock group through Europe, so he is not alien to the stage, while Liston was an old con man whose motives were more shrouded and whose character more opaque than Ali's himself. "Can he kiss a bullet?" asked Liston—suggesting that there was a poet inside the Ugly Bear. Ali's favorite white sparring partner is, of course, Howard Cosell, the ham of hams, a tube creation equal to his opponent.

Ali's acting is at the heart of the mystery, and goes much deeper than fear. He acts so much that, like the girl in the red shoes, he cannot stop; nor perhaps can he tell whether he's doing it or not. The solemn measured voice that alternates with the rant is a species of counterpoint, to keep you (and him) from getting bored. Since he can only do monologues, he must do them in several voices: like God, talking to himself. Anyone who can even make his blood pressure perform is no mean actor.

Again, we return to Louisville for clues. And we find to no one's surprise that Cassius, Sr. is also a non-stop performer. Ali would not be the first great man to love his mother while imitating his father (actually, he claims to love them both, and I suspect he does—but this need not exclude a deadly rivalry). This may be what bothered Plimpton: that he was doing his father's act, raging and boasting, although his face and soul belonged to his mother. This being the kind of theory that athletes gaze at, quite rightly, in stupefaction, we'll pass on quickly. At any rate, there's no doubt he got the act, or at least the germs of it, from his father. Outside of the endless acting elder Negroes had to do in a white world, to the sometime derision of their children, Mr. Clay has taken a turn at street-singing and is a master of the bragging monologue ("I am the greatest" is *his* line), delivered in a staccato jumble. According to the invaluable Olsen, Mr. Clay has even passed as an Arab complete with shawls, tassels and a mysterious past—which might have given young Ali ideas. Ironically, as we shall see, the old Arab impersonator came to hate the Black Muslims when they fixed their grip on his son and Cassius, Jr. took to wearing a fez for real.

From the first, Mr. Clay has tried to claim a piece of Ali's career; to make it seem like a joint operation, all of which Ali views with thinly veiled irritation. John Cottrell quotes him: "If I had a child who got rich and famous, I know I'd want to cash in too, like my daddy . . . But listen here. Who made me is me." Yet there always has been a mentor or substitute father around, and Mr. Clay has battled every one of them. First the kindly cop Joe Martin who must have taught Ali something ("he was just like any other 12-year-old").

Mr. Clay fought to keep Martin from becoming Ali's first professional manager, which Martin seems to view now without rancor. (It is a striking feature of Ali's career that he leaves so little ill feeling in his tempestuous wake). Later, Ali was taken in tow by a group of white Louisville businessmen, and again Cassius, Sr. fought them to exhaustion over minute contractual points. "The greatest contract ever written was written by Cassius Clay, Senior," he told Olsen. "I'm a money man. I'm crazy for money." And to underline the point, he asked to be paid for the interview.

Meanwhile, though, the Daddy of Daddies, Elijah Muhammad himself, was waiting in the wings. Details of Ali's conversion are vague: it is likely that his brother Rachaman (christened Rudolph, and later re-christened Rudolph Valentino by his brother), heard the word first. What is significant in terms of family politics and the primal grapple is that Ali announced it in the morning after he won the championship against Liston. His most hysterical scenes to date occurred before and after this fight, and it could be that they had little to do with the fight. Ali was on a spiritual tear and burning to tell about his rebirth. Thus, at the moment when Cassius, Sr. was most likely to move in and smear himself in glory, claiming his share of the crown, Ali cut him off at the knees by changing his own name. No wonder he stood in the ring screaming "I am the greatest"—his father's old phrase—until he seemed really demented.

The name change seems to have had considerable symbolic importance to Cassius, Sr. "I wouldn't change my name for anybody," Mr. Clay shouts at Olsen. "He's trying to rub that name out and I'm trying

57

to make it strong." Mr. Clay had planned on making a fortune in advertising, and he proceeds grimly with his diminished designs for "Cassius Clay Enterprises," which would have blanketed Louisville. Later, Ali will buy some kind of a cocktail lounge for his father to run, and it will fail, but by then the battle is over and there is no question who is doing whom a favor.

Again, this is from the outside. When I meet the real people later in the book they may seem entirely different and the myth will blow away. But sticking only to the texts, we find that Ali's new father Elijah not only renamed him, effacing all trace of Cassius, Sr., but forbade him even to talk to his earthly father. And Ali abided by this, sending messages through his mother, until the link was severed. Since then, the old man has done some sensational lettering for Ali's training camp in the Poconos (neither father nor son can spell worth a damn), and the family unit is serene and unruffled again. Guess what you can from the sharp shrewd face of the father and the gentle amiability of the mother. Ali swears he had a happy childhood, and nobody is about to disagree. His passion for display does not include *any* revelations of consequence; in fact, it seems designed expressly to hide them. His friend Jose Torres passes on the authorized view that Ali and his old man were always the best of buddies, and strangely I do not find this incompatible. When a father gets that close, he can inflict more pain.

Since most childhoods are immeasurably happy *and* unhappy, it's a surly writer who won't let the subject have the kind he wants. However, one thing about Ali's boyhood continues to nag me. Why didn't he learn to read and write? The usual

explanation is that he was too wrapped up in boxing. But this was only from the age of 12 on. Most people have mastered reading by then, if they're going to.

Unfortunately there's no one left to ask. Everyone who knew him has been questioned to death by now. There is no point searching for the Missing Aunt who knows everything. All the aunts have been accounted for. Our passion for interrogation has left no relative unturned. It seems that Cassius was just an irrepressively playful kid who ran alongside the school bus instead of getting in, and who set local hooky records from the first grade on. Whether there was some deep resistance to learning, based on some unplayful sense of rebellion, or whether it was a mechanical difficulty, we'll never know. What we do know is that his brother, Rachaman, doesn't read or write very well either.

To all intents and purposes, Cassius was born at the age of 12, the day he entered the gym and started fighting. From then on, he was relatively pampered, like a stage brat. ("I've never worked a day in my life.") At the age when the George Foremans of this world are learning their trade in alleys and bars, Cassius was the toast of the Louisville gym. Although he would later bear the black man's burden against an old mill-hand like Frazier, his early years had little in common with black experience. If it wasn't exactly Judy Garland's childhood, it was enough to make him excessively brash and sassy for a prizefighter.

Brash enough to bounce into Angelo Dundee's gym in 1959, *before* the Rome Olympics, and demand to be trained by him; brash enough to spar with Dundee's ace, Willie Pastrano, the light-heavyweight champion, and give a good account of him-

59

self. Then, after the Olympics, he invades Ingemar Johansson's camp, and offers to take on the heavyweight champion himself. For two rounds he makes an ass out of the apoplectic Swede and practically has to be spirited out of camp . . . but only after telling the world he's going to be the next champ—the youngest champ in history, no less.

There can't be anything bothering this kid, can there? A news film shot around then shows Cassius sitting in a convertible with some fellow dudes, beating out time and letting things shake, like any young guy who's got it made. A closer look shows that he's imitating swinging rather than actually swinging, but at least he thinks it's a good image. Later, he has a high old time sassing Sonny Liston at Las Vegas. Sonny threatens some minor form of mutilation and Ali flees the crap table in terror; "darn right I was scared" he admits, laughing. He's still riding all the machines in playland—you can almost hear the maniac shrieks of the roller coaster, and the groans of the ghost house. And at night, Torres reports some tomcatting around Miami, to complete the fun-house cycle. Yet this blithe spirit will soon be entering the somber world of Elijah Muhammad. Why? Nobody ever entered the Muslims for laughs.

Because it makes no sense, the writers don't know how to take his conversion. Since the only constant in his life so far has been self-promotion they tend to ascribe it mostly to that. The older ones continue petulantly to call him Clay, like his daddy (I guess they'd call St. Paul, Saul and Pope John, Angie Roncallo) and then some fighters like Ernie Terrell pick this up to taunt him and sell tickets, and in no time a quite serious matter has become hopelessly entwined with promotional imperatives. Floyd Patterson declares that he will bring the title "back to America," and denounces the Muslims from his Catholic perch. Well, surely Old Floyd is serious, isn't he?

Ali seems to think so, and subjects the pensive old champion to a prolonged beating. Yet it still smells of hype. We have seen too many of these trumped-up feuds, and not one of them has ever hurt the gate. An occasional sincere one makes it all the better. But what is sincerity by now in this prince of actors? His nervous system mimes rage so well that it becomes real like an old actor's tears. But is he really mad at dear old Floyd? (It would be hard to manage.) Or does he, like a method actor, think of something else and get mad at that? Or does he just start shouting and follow his voice? Watching him again after the first Liston fight, haranguing the bemused boxing world in his greatest apocalypse yet, one senses the body carrying him, creating its own excitement, like a pentacostalist's. Let's see what my mouth says next. Follow the flapping jaw.

Anyway, his religion had not been tested yet. Muslimism is something of a mystery sect anyway, well suited to Ali's temperament; like him, it is both noisy and secretive. "Elijah speaks" screams the Muslim paper. But what does he say? His edicts are elliptical. His face is guarded. It may have been photographed more often than Ali's (his newspaper is punctuated by it), yet always in the same expression. Even now that he's dead he seems as alive as he did then, and he still speaks. Maximum uproar, minimal disclosure. Ali has found a home.

His personal guru is Malcolm X, which

is like being baptized by St. Paul himself. Malcolm X is the most brilliant of Muslims, but he proceeds to soar too high. He criticizes the master, Elijah, allegedly for his swinging sex life, and is criticized back for saying "the chickens have come home to roost" after Kennedy's assassination. (It's OK for a Muslim to have a private cackle over white men's misfortunes, but publicly one should be as impassive as Elijah; Ali himself will later be advised to cool his racism slightly after the Terrell fight.)

Secret organizations produce the juiciest rumors, and the exact details of Malcolm's assassination may never be known. But we do know that he set up his own splinter group, and that Ali did not follow him. Although he still uses phrases of Malcolm's and carries his intellectual imprint more than anyone's, he declared then that "Elijah is the wisest" and did not turn a hair when his patron was killed. "You just don't buck Mr. Muhammad and get away with it," he told *Playboy.* "I don't want to talk about him anymore."

"We are not disturbed because we are innocent," said Elijah, and this may have been true. The killers may have been freelance Muslims or (a black friend suggests impishly) FBI agents. What strikes a chill, in me if not Ali, is that Malcolm himself said, "I live like a man who's already dead. No one can get out of the Black Muslims without trouble," just before they got him.

Elijah himself always preached nonviolence, but so many of his followers were and are ex-convicts and such that violence always broods in the air. It doesn't hurt their effectiveness and they are certainly not the first religion to have it both ways.

Anyway the laughing boy image still prevails in those pre-draft-board days, and

in no time the incident is turned into ragtime. Gossip has it that 300 of Malcolm's followers will be gunning for Ali at the second Liston fight, in Lewiston, Maine. But then gossip also has it that Elijah's followers are threatening Liston and getting him to dump the fight. What the hell, it's all good for business. A P.R. man leaks a story about a sniper in the stadium and the astute sportswriter, Jimmy Cannon, for once falls for it, and the story appears on page one of the *Journal American.* It may help a little to sell this turkey of a fight.

In becoming a Muslim, Ali guarantees that his aim in life will always be achieved, if he runs out of the energy to do it himself: that is, he will always be the villain, the black man, in every fight: people everywhere will scream for his scalp and suffer agonies of frustration when they don't get it. There is money in this, of course, but also some strange personal satisfaction—as if this were his natural role, the thing he was born to do: to escape a howling crowd,

Ali with Malcolm X.

to defy it with his art, to go home safely to his own people.

A dangerous game, as it turns out. Ali perhaps did not gauge how much he was enraging the crowd, or how little sense of humor some people have. He might be acting, but they were not; and when he completed his Muslim manifesto by defying the draft and saying "I ain't got nothing against them Viet Congs," he added the finishing touch. This pleasant, good-hearted popinjay became one of the most hated men in America.

But for all the friends he lost, he gained some too—for starters, 600 million Muslims (if you can believe Asian statistics), including shahs and princes from all over. A fair exchange for a man of vision. Ali had already been to Africa and evidently liked what he saw: an untapped continent of love. White Americans may be unaware that Islam is the last of the world's great growth religions, with a most insinuating charm— particularly for men. Ali's conversion to it might be compared to an Englishman's conversion to Catholicism: the comrades he loses domestically, he more than makes up for overseas.

In the non-stop play in Ali's head, he needs cheers as well as boos; he must be hero and villain and clown all at once. And he doesn't have to go abroad when the mood for applause comes on. There are mosques in over 50 American cities, and the promise of fraternity that goes with Muslimism in all of them. Ali's training camp in the Poconos is reported to be as friendly and cheerful as a camp can be. (We shall see: at this writing, he is about to start training for one Chuck Wepner, otherwise known as the Bayonne Bleeder. It is a match-up that would have amused Jack Johnson: Wepner cuts on sight.)

Right now, I am curious as to how they manage to be both cheerful and secretive— but not too curious. A church where they search you for concealed weapons on the way in is not your average religion. So for reasons of health, I am happy to take them at face value—whatever that is.

The Muslims' most striking characteristic is their aloneness. Elijah was not just another black leader, but an end in himself, and his followers are not simply representative blacks. Later, when I ask Ali how he selects his charities, he will tell me "I give only to Muslim charities." It is a closed world even within the black world.

As a Catholic raised in the One True Church I understand what a scandal this is to others. The image of the Muslims is one of overweening arrogance, like unto the Pope's, and it was this that Ali was plugging into.

The Black Muslims are not only at odds with white society, but with black Christians like Patterson and with black integrationists of all kinds. They are even considered something of an aberration by the Islam center in New York, because of their racism.

In the shifting politics of black power, a certain reputation for mystery and even gangsterism may do no harm. And the Muslims are a natural for it. Islam is a warrior religion to begin with and there is even an Italian superstition that the Mafia is of Arab origin, so it is easy to view them as a private group capable of terrorism. Justice Thurgood Marshall even thought back in 1959 that they were financed by General Nasser. And Malcolm accused them in his last frantic days of allying with the Nazi party and the Klan for their own fiendish purposes. So one rumor seems to fit them as well as another.

On top of this, even many black brothers don't know who's Muslim and who isn't. This makes for even more menace. Their presence is felt in black neighborhoods, but it is hard to measure. And since no one can count them, a few bodies can go a long way. A black friend tells me that they may approach you quietly for recruitment, but outside of that he isn't sure who they are and what they're doing. He adds that he thinks they're probably a good thing.

In some respects, they certainly are. For one thing they act as a sort of Convicts Anonymous. Hardened criminals who laugh at social workers listen to them with respect; pimps and winos give up drinking and smoking at their request. Their rate of drug rehabilitation soars above the next competitor's. No one since Carrie Nation has cleaned up a neighborhood so successfully.

The catch, if you call it that, is that they have to offer their sinners something in return. And what they offer them is enormous personal prosperity. They have to show the thieves and muggers that there's money in the boy scout virtues; and they have to show the dudes that it pays to dress like an undertaker. It takes a lot of very visible results to do that.

Hence their non-stop emphasis on how well they're doing—and hence partly their appeal to Ali, a kid who grew up boasting and listening to boasting. But for him, unlike the pimps and cons, the puritan rules seem to have held at least as much attraction as the dough—although at first glance you would hardly suppose he needed them. Ali appears to be one of nature's puritans,

not just in regard to such trivia as drinking and smoking, but in his whole use of time and energy. Before his enforced layoff, he was always in training; nowadays, he has a little trouble with the pastry tray, but considerably less than, say, King Farouk. A sweet tooth is the last weakness Muslims can help you with.

Hardly the kind of demoralized black man the Muslims are accustomed to putting back on his feet. In fact their only noticeable contribution to Ali's morals was convincing him to divorce his first wife, Sonji, who wore mini-skirts, and to settle down with a nice Muslim girl and raise a family. "The Muslims have stolen my man's mind," said Sonji, echoing Malcolm X. Sonji herself was a Muslim, but apparently not Muslim enough.

There is something disturbing to the liberal mind about a man so thoroughly converted that he virtually has his wife chosen for him, if that's what happened. But maybe he would have wanted to give respectability a whirl anyway at some point in his acting career; maybe he saw a Sidney Poitier movie around then and decided to outsquare the champion. Anyway, the Muslim code gave him the starch he needed to withstand his uproarious appetites and for a while he became such a monster of virtue that he laid an impossible moral burden on himself. Nowadays, if he wants to go back to flirting with stray foxes, no one is going to hold it against him—neither the pressmen, who have their own lives to lead, nor apparently the Muslims themselves.

If Ali were to develop a taste for white girls (it goes without saying there are rumors about this as about everything), that would be another story. The Muslims are

implacable about racial separation, and in fact this is the aspect that has done most to define the new Ali. Cassius Clay had been a separatist too, going along politely with Jim Crow and not butting in where he wasn't wanted. But his feelings cannot have been simple.

His father's views veered radically, as we have seen, between hating the whites and accommodating them. After all, he was thought to be descended from the great Henry Clay, and it was hard to boast about that in the same breath in which one lashed the oppressors. The original Cassius Marcellus Clay was one of the very few slave-owning abolitionists, and is known to have boxed with a slave named George—who knows, maybe Ali's ancestor. So ambiguity was built into the family.

As for his mother, Odessa Grady Clay, she was quarter-Irish, and bequeathed him his fair skin. (I even thought of claiming him for the great Irish heavyweights, but that goes a bit far.) When he announced his conversion, she said that his white Louisville backers "should have protected him" from the Muslims—a fair tip-off to her sense of who does what for whom in the racial hierarchy.

Ali's own instincts have a right to be tangled, and no white man is likely to find out what they really are. What one does know is that rebels, whether Sean Mac-Stiofain of the IRA or Patty Hearst of the Symbionese Army, are likely to have a strong dash of the enemy in them (Mac-Stiofain is almost totally English). It takes one to know one. Ali talks jokingly, obsessively about "niggers" and while he was in Zaire, he allegedly told reporters that the girls could use some white blood for their looks.

65

By his conversion, Ali settled any doubts he may have had about his racial loyalties. He would be reborn as one man, not two. Most blacks do not have this choice, or burden, as you prefer. No black boxer ever had a better shot at full color-blind acceptance by the white community; none had less of the ghetto or the cotton-field about him. So it took some doing to get a white audience to root against him in favor of an archetypal menace like Liston.

Why did he do it? If pressed, he can dredge up a couple of racist incidents that he witnessed as a child, but they pale beside the help he received from Sgt. Martin and the Louisville Santas. Maybe it was the *help* he resents, but if so he showed no sign of it at the time. The young man who danced into Rome and "could have been elected President" by the Olympic team (white votes included) had no visible racial scars. In becoming a Muslim he was taking on the scars of his brothers—and of his father too, whether his old man liked it or not.

The immediate circumstance of his conversion seems to have been in Miami as the Liston fight loomed, although some Ali-watchers place it earlier. Just to judge

Ali and Wallace Muhammad at left;
Elijah Muhammad at far right.

from the graph of his love life, as depicted by Torres, the later date makes more sense. In the fight world you either run with the whores and pimps or you find something else—a choice that most fighters find easy enough to make. But Cassius had not yet shaken off his early religious training. As the championship approached, perhaps he wanted to be worthy of it. In the heat and pressure of Miami, he sought righteousness, and he found it improbably in the Muslims, the street gang gone straight, or fairly straight.

There he joined his younger brother Rachaman, for whom he had always felt a near maternal tenderness, and maybe Rachaman was attraction enough. The actual go-between was a legendary figure called Cap'n Sam who shined shoes and touted racehorses (although the Muslims forbid gambling for their own members). Cap'n Sam is someone else we don't talk about now. Like Malcolm, he vanished from Ali's history like a puff of smoke. But he was the most visible symbol of the raffish puritans that Ali had chosen to identify with.

Now with Elijah as his father and Malcolm as his blood brother, he had an alternative to gangsters like Blinky Palermo (Liston's *capo*) and the other sharks who infest the game, plus a spiritual ideal that did not involve returning hang-dog to his childhood.

Whatever one feels about the church he joined, this decision had its noble side. Granted that it was faddish, and even prudent to acclaim one's blackness at the time and that even the obliging Sammy Davis was murmuring stray nothings about the brothers; granted also that Ali is not immune to fads: still, he did not have to go

68

Peace rally, 1968.

this far—and as mentioned, it cost him.

Early interviews with Clay indicate an interest in money almost equal to his father's: it is one of the great abstractions that seize artists' souls even more than the rest of us. Now he was renouncing it like the rich young man in the Bible. He even took a vow of poverty—whatever precisely that means. (The Muslims remind me slightly of the Opus Dei, a Spanish Catholic outfit, also very hush hush, who have a vow of poverty that simply means "spiritual" poverty, which even I could handle.) Anyway, the boxing authorities took him up on it by banning him from his livelihood.

There is no doubt that the conversion was genuine in his own special sense of the word. It took some swallowing at first because Ali always takes some swallowing, and because the teachings of Black Islam are so bizarre. Elijah taught among other things that a villainous fellow called Dr. Yakub one day grafted the white race off the black and shouted it to 6,000 years of supremacy which is just drawing to a close. Meanwhile there's a spaceship full of black men out there waiting to pounce and liquidate us all, to be followed by an era of black supremacy.

Ali wanted the religion so badly that he bought the whole crock—so long as Elijah taught it. (I'll try to ask him what he would do if the brass suddenly said, "no more spaceship.") He grimly went about learning his new faith and reciting it, like other Muslims, rather woodenly, as if he had a gun in his back. The woodenness made people all the more suspicious. But this route is not unfamiliar among converts. Cynicism about his sincerity came mostly from those unfamiliar or unsympathetic with religious experience. Ali was a

70

preacher with world responsibilities, and he wanted to get things right. So he wrote his speeches out laboriously on cue cards (he is not a man of letters) and memorized them. Many a young priest has done the same thing.

Anyway, the media creature had gone serious on us and no one knew what to make of it, at least through the years of his first championship, from Liston to draft board. He prayed to Allah five times a day and denounced the poisons in white men's food (lobster was the swine of the sea, it turned out) and he went along with Elijah's dictum that white men are blue-eyed devils, which was going some for a promotional stunt even in the big-mouthed sixties.

Still, the put-on style was so ingrained, and white irritation was so profitable, that we couldn't quite believe his Muslim apprenticeship until, in 1967, he politely declined to step forward at the Houston draft center and serve his country at its dirtiest hour.

Maybe he became serious for the first time at that moment. There is no evidence he'd cared about the war up to then. "I ain't got nothing against them Viet Congs" was an innocent country-style remark and not the work of the devil. Later, he would visit student groups and, like Jack Johnson, visit Europe where he was lionized, and he may have picked up some foreign policy tips. But he still refused to have any peacenik bunting at his meetings, or to be associated with the peace movement in any way. He was against *all* wars, not just this one; he had nothing against them Saigonese either.

This is what his young followers still find hard to face, as they doggedly insist he is one of them. Ali's decision was religious, not political, and the religion in question is stringent, archaic and uncompromising. Its Eastern affiliations may have looked exotic to them, but this is the folly of distance. The American nation of Islam has actually squeezed the glamor out of the original until it looks more like a Quaker prayer meeting. Elijah kept only the hard parts, and doubled them and threw in the heresy of racism. And Ali accepts it all. Even when he was suspended by Elijah in 1970, he adhered to the dietary laws. Perhaps this is why a ramshackle Catholic like myself is impressed by his conversion, and refuses to take it as a joke. If it becomes one later, as we change reels, that's another story.

What does a celebrity do in a mystery religion? Acts mysterious, of course—but then what? It barely showed in his boxing, though some observers claimed to see signs. Strange birds of passage began to appear in his corner, along with the white devils, Dundee and Dr. Pacheco, whom he wisely insisted on keeping. In his fight with the armor-plated George Chuvalo of Canada, *Sports Illustrated* reported that he was taking advice from Muslims like Cap'n Sam Saxon and his new manager, Herbert Muhammad, instead of Dundee, and it appeared possible, although no one ever looked good wearing out their hands on Chuvalo. Then, against the German Karl Mildenberger, he fought exactly the way you're not supposed to fight lefthanders, moving clockwise into the right leads—a sheer lapse of memory, since he'd practiced it right all month.

It is possible that the pinpoint concentration required by professional boxing, the kind so finely tuned that the wrong breakfast can spoil it, was suffering slightly from his new ministry—especially if he was "teaching and preaching and fishing for converts 160 hours a week," as Elijah testified to the draft board.

But if so, he shook it off like a head cold, and came back as sharp as ever against Cleveland Williams, in one of his most elegant fights. It takes a lot to get Ali down. The authorities were already nibbling away at his championship as he fought his last great fights against Terrell and Folley. But Ali the boxer seems totally untouched by the real world. In 1966, the Muslims suspended his chauffeur and his valet, possibly just to get his attention, and forbade him from driving his Cadillac for a while, but even the gnomic Elijah couldn't check his ebullience. In a film shot around then called *Float Like a Butterfly, Sting Like a Bee*, we see the last of the old Ali; he is still surrounded by his claque, merry fellows all, and the scene resounds with the smug exuberance of the counter-culture. *We'll lick the establishment, we'll lick the Man; oh yeah*, as if they were really going somewhere.

So the Man balled up his withered fist and let him have it. The other sixties' rebels would get theirs later, from the cops in Chicago and the storm troopers at Attica—good rebels and bad, Berrigans and Weathermen, the whole crazy quilt coalition—but as usual, Ali led the way. The laughter died around him and the hangers-on drifted away, to hang on to someone else and crowd round a fresh flame, and to be replaced by scroungers—anyone calling himself a Muslim was good for a touch—and a few good friends, like Bundini and Howard Cosell and millions of liberal supporters. He was not physically alone, any more than Nixon at San Clemente; he had only,

like Nixon, lost his title, and his whole reason for living from age 12 on.

During his semi-official suspension, Ali could probably have dredged up a few fights in out-of-the-way places, the way Jack Johnson had when he was on the run. But with the title out of reach, this quickly becomes a squirrel cage. The championship is what boxing is all about; otherwise it is all exhibitions and nobody ever fought a great exhibition. No politician out of office ever unraveled faster than a boxer banned from a title. With nothing to aim at he might very well have slipped more and more, like a black jazz-man in Paris—or like Jack Johnson himself, on his way to the flea circus. A total ban was better than this.

So began his three years of exile within his own country, years in which he grew into his new name and into a personality worth writing a book about. Comparing him with Frank Sinatra may seem like bathos at this point, as the old hood sinks further into his religion of self-congratula-

Ali in Cairo mosque.

73

tion—"I did it my way," what a creed to wind up with. A baby could say as much after finger-painting the bathroom. But in the years when Sinatra lost his voice and his girl, he became an interesting man.

Ali's energy problem could have pushed him in a hundred different directions, most of them bad. It did push him into a habit of aimless driving from city to city, and of frequent street raps with his people in which he could wallow as martyr-king. But fortunately, the Muslims gave him a real frame to work in as well. Like many famous converts, from St. Augustine to Thomas Merton, Ali seemed to relish surrendering his flaming ego to a higher authority. He would not just be obedient: he would be the *most* obedient. If family life with a nice Muslim girl was indicated, he would be the greatest family man of all time. Pictures appeared of him in *Ebony* magazine romping with his children, or sitting serenely with his demure wife Belinda. Never *was* so much domesticity.

At the same time, he hit the lecture circuit with equal intensity. In Christian theology the venial sin of vanity is the opposite of the mortal sin of pride, and I think of that as I read about Ali's new endeavors. He wanted to look good, but he had no illusions about himself. He applied himself humbly to the preaching trade, enlisting his wife's help in writing out those cue cards and adding slowly to his list of sermons. He might ad lib during the question period, but he had too much respect for the preacher's art to trust his clever tongue all the way. Later, when he took his show to Broadway, in the form of a musical called *Buck White,* the critics unanimously praised his unassuming modesty—not bad for the world's greatest braggart.

In fact, the only harsh review I saw (from Walter Kerr) accused him of being too nice. The original version of *Buck White* had been a vehicle for black rage: Buck stands on stage, whipping up the brothers and disposing of a planted white heckler, etc. But Ali brought such sweetness to the part that Mr. Kerr charged him with exploiting black rage without really feeling it.

When Ali the actor tries to actually act, his feelings become well and truly impenetrable. And I'm told he tried to imitate Olivier or some such, which clouds things further. But surely he could mime black rage at that particular time of his life. Or was it beyond any actor? Unfortunately, black rhetoric, which had hit the country with such hurricane force a few years earlier, was a very worn-out coin by the late sixties. Everyone was using it, so it was impossible to tell who was meaning it. So perhaps Ali the enigma was simply a hopeless instrument for expressing rage—if that was really what he was trying to do. He had faked this emotion so often, in his fun-filled early career, that even a serious Ali sets us laughing now.

But was he ever really angry? When I step inside the mirror I may ask him—though I might as well expect a straight answer from the Red Queen in the original *Alice Through the Looking Glass.* It is my impression from out here that the Black Muslims as such were not above exploiting anti-white rage if it got people into the tent, but that was not their first order of business. It always helps to have an enemy, but the real task was setting the blacks' own house in order.

So Ali directed himself to the "nee-grow"—the black man who had been demoralized by American life and had lost his African dignity. But Ali does not mean quite what white people might expect by the word "nee-grow." Stepin Fetchit, the shuffling darky of the old movies, is a close friend of Ali's, and his good-luck charm, Bundini Brown, is the very model of the ingratiating black entertainer. If he turned up in a white man's movie, black groups would picket. On the other hand, Ali despises Afro hairdos, the basic symbol of young black independence. "Afros are a nee-grow invention," he tells *Ebony*. "Africans don't wear no Afros."

Once again, this hero of a freaked-out generation confounds his followers. Stepin Fetchit is more to his taste than Rap Brown or Stokely or even his *own followers*—the flashy young dudes in the Afros and the fancy threads, who are all show and no performance. Ali's deepest contempt, I would surmise, is for blacks who don't work for a living, and who spend more time on their hair than they do on their women and children. It is just one more paradox of this symbol of vanity and self-centered youth that he only owned about three suits until recently. (His father, of an earlier vintage, has always been a snappy dresser.)

Whatever their origins, the Muslims that Ali joined saw themselves as an elite and rather conservative corps, calculated to attract some fastidious element in his own temperament. In some ways, the top people were almost a parody of white businessmen. Even their zany side, the ponderous ritual and the spaceship is not so far from the carryings-on of certain white masonic groups. Big businessmen, from J. P. Morgan on down, have been notoriously superstitious, and it may be no coincidence that they also turn to the Middle East, especially Egypt, for their symbols, or that Elijah Mu-

hammad's fez would look very well in a Shriners' parade.

So this was no swinging black power organization that Ali was joining, but something closer to a masonic lodge—at least at the summit: things get rougher lower down. Its motto, like Calvinism's, could be "Allah helps those who help themselves." He rewards His followers with supermarkets up to 70 times 7. The Muslims in turn were recruiting a very powerful center of black capitalism—the heavyweight champion of the world. Religions are as hung-up on celebrities as anyone.

The only catch about Ali as a center of black capitalism was that Ali made his money in sports, which Elijah had officially denounced. Since sports is the opium of the underdog, this was not unreasonable. But surely, he could make an exception for Ali, who was so much more than a sportsman.

Unfortunately, the late Elijah could not make exceptions easily. As the last messenger of Allah, he was infallible or nothing, and a prophet cannot eat his words. So Ali entered the church as a good-bad boy—something again familiar to Catholics, who have watched divorced luminaries come and go. A curious and tortuous relationship with the Muslims ensued, which has dominated Ali's life to the present moment.

In Act One, before the draft board brought the curtain down, Ali's boxing seems to have been tolerated on high: Elijah's son Herbert became his manager and he phased out his business with the white businessmen of Louisville. The details are as dull as such details usually are. But it seems that Ali was willing to maintain the Louisville connection, while giving them a smaller rake-off and a smaller voice in his affairs. They, in turn, felt that he was getting rotten advice from his new management and they declined to renew his contract. A fellow in Ali's camp says it was the other way round. It doesn't much matter. It seems quite in keeping with the amiable Ali that even in the throes of conversion he'd be quite willing to go along with two sets of managers.

In the movie *Float Like a Butterfly Sting Like a Bee,* there is a scene showing the Louisville syndicate chuckling over Ali, and there is a hint in it of "look at that ungrateful darky, after all we've done for it." But the film is propagandistically shot and mounted, and it ignores the facts that, a) they had a right to be sore regardless of color. Having staked Ali to several years of trouble-free security in which to develop his art, they had not tried to cash in unduly except in smugness and, b) they insisted on keeping a trust fund of $50,000 for his 35th birthday, in case his new advisers ruined him. In all this, they probably were in full harmony with Cassius, Sr., the first of Ali's fathers. Herbert Muhammad the diplomat now says that he himself went to them for advice in the early going; but then you won't hear Herbert saying many bad things about white businessmen these days.

The point is that Ali himself did not create any bad feeling. He had people do that for him now. He had become an object for others to fight over, and all kinds of uproar was possible without his having to take any part at all. A nice position for a vain, passive man if he has that side.

To what extent was he still his own man at this point and to what extent a vociferous pawn? Opinions differ drastically on this, but it is worth noting that Malcolm X, a fellow media creature (it took nothing less to convert Ali) with an enormous personal following, lost his power and his life the moment he split from Elijah. Without an organization, he was nothing. And this must have impressed Ali as he faced the Houston draft board: a panel of good old boys, every bit as menacing as any street gang or board of businessmen.

Ali's pacifism was very much a Muslim production: there is no hint that he'd ever had such ideas himself. And if they were indeed stage managing him, they made no effort to spare their boy hardship. There was a foolish theory running round, worthy of the Watergate White House, that Ali did not wish to expose his pretty face to the rigors of Army life; but an equal and opposite one had it that the Army would have let him waltz through his service, fighting exhibitions like Joe Louis and being a hawk by implication. Surely even Washington in its majestic dimness did not want a showdown with Ali's following.

If a deal was offered, it was not accepted. Elijah had sweated out World War II in jail for encouraging conscientious objection, and his disciple would do no less. Maybe you could hang loose on the other doctrines, but this one about fighting white men's wars was central. Elijah testified eloquently on behalf of Ali's ministry, and Ali prepared his own mind for prison. Rapping in his best free association style, he talked lightly of all the brothers he'd run into in the Slam. After all those years in training camp, prison life would be a snap, and he might get some studying done in there. Airy talk, perhaps, but since the first Frazier fight, people have been less anxious to look for signs of weakness and cowardice in Ali.

So the decision the flower-children applauded so rapturously originated with an organization which despised them and pre-

78

ferred even then to deal with their businessman parents. It is a tribute to Ali's charisma that it came across as an act of universal benevolence. Perhaps in some way it was. As for him, the experience bound him ever closer to his new religion. Even the bravest conscientious objectors tend to have a heavy dependence on their co-believers and Ali now had nothing but his Muslim identity to fall back on. Such dependence and willingness to serve are irresistible to religious leaders, and Elijah proceeded to chasten Ali as many a Pope has chastened a saint. Just as Ali's fortunes began to look up, and it appeared that his exile might be ending, he found himself suspended from the Muslims and from the use of his precious new name.

It all began on a Howard Cosell program in 1969, when one Mouth asked the other if he would like to fight again and Ali answered, sure, he needed the money. The message came back swiftly from the Mountain: "I want the world to know that Muhammad Ali has stepped down off the spiritual platform of Islam . . . we, the Muslims, are not with Muhammad Ali in his desire to work in the sports for the sake of a 'leetle' money." The tone is interesting: that kind of sarcasm with a heavyweight champion suggests an absolutely secure patriarchal ascendancy based on love or power or psychological dependence. Elijah is, to borrow Ali's phrase, "spanking me like my daddy."

Ali took it without blinking, but worse was to come: "We shall call him Cassius Clay. We take away the name of Allah from him until he proves himself worthy of that name." In fact, Muhammad Ali is not just a name, it's a title, meaning "worthy of respect" and "beloved of Allah"—the best

you can get. And this title too, the symbol of his rebirth, was being snatched back by his spiritual father.

Does Ali *like* this kind of spanking? Or is it a charade that we outsiders do not understand? As it turned out, Ali clung to his new name throughout his suspension, though he wasn't entitled to it. The bigots who called him Cassius Clay were right for a change; they were following Elijah's instructions.

How serious was the suspension anyway? The signs point both ways as usual. For a full year, Muslims were ordered to have nothing to do with Ali—and most of them didn't. Even his inseparable brother Rachaman stayed away from the set of *Buck White*. Then again, his manager Herbert Muhammad hung around, and was duly suspended himself. This sounds serious, but Elijah's relations with his sons are an enigma wrapped in a riddle. Herbert is still in boxing, he is still a power in the Muslims and at no point has he seemed spiritually tormented. But then, he is also a guarded man, smooth as silk, who could beat Sidney Greenstreet himself to the bird that dreams are made of.

Ali's offense, as he explained to puzzled observers like Bob Lipsyte of the *Times,* was not fighting itself, but admitting he needed the money. Allah is supposed to take care of that, if you are faithful. Boxing is a peccadillo in contrast, like bingo. In fact, the Almighty might even take a hand in it if the cause is just. After the first Liston fight, Elijah spoke to his new disciple as follows: "You tell it, dear apostle. White people wanted Liston to beat up and probably kill poor little Clay. But Allah and myself said no. This assured his victory."

With such cornermen, any religion would seem attractive, and Ali made sure he kept at least one of the two. Since he was on the outs with Elijah, he intensified his devotion to Allah to the point where he seemed able to call upon him at will. This would come in handy against the likes of Frazier and Foreman. In fact, before the Foreman fight, Ali stressed his dependence on Allah so much that some observers (including me) thought that he was throwing in the towel. Fighters who expect the Almighty to bail them out have a dismal record.

But, of course, this is no ordinary fighter. Ali's psychological apparatus is in the walk-on-water class, even with those heavy Negro bones; and an act of faith, even half serious, becomes next thing to a fact. Against Frazier, he willed himself up off the canvas, when he was by all normal standards unconscious, and against Foreman, he willed his way into the body of a younger man—himself at 23. Does he really believe Allah does it? Let's say it beats a rabbit foot.

This gimmicky use of religion is familiar to Catholic football teams: if our harshly whispered Hail Marys did not reassure us, they might at least rattle the enemy. But it should be noted that Ali's faith seems to have developed during the years he wasn't fighting. It isn't something you can turn on and off for an evening. Religious masters like Pascal have suggested that you must practice a faith *before* you get it; i.e., first you pray, and then you believe.

This would suit Ali's temperament fine. He likes nothing better than to take a piece of make-believe and will it into reality. For instance, he has been known to act out a whole fight in advance (maybe not quite

80

what Pascal had in mind) and then convince himself that this is how the real fight will go. If it doesn't, he convinces himself just as firmly that he had planned something else all along. For instance, the punch that knocked out Liston in Lewiston, one of the great accidents of our time, became the next day his special "Anchor Punch," the knock-out secret of the Aztecs or the Watusi.

Obviously such a man could make a formidable spiritual leader. Anyone who can will the future or, failing that, invent the past is in business. The great Father Divine got his break when a judge who had sentenced him dropped dead, and Father said, "I sure hated to do it." Ali, if less spectacular than that, is the closest thing to a miracle worker the Muslims had. Elijah's recent death caused speculation that the champ's time had come and that he could now do a little spanking himself; but apparently not. For all his quirky gifts, Ali has always been managed by someone else—and perhaps he always will be. There is a dependent strain beneath the self-assertion, an insatiable need for daddies, and he may prefer to remain the brilliantly effective tool of someone else. Watch the hooded gaze for clues: he may have grown a real ego under the fake one.

Anyway, Ali prepared for his ministry during his exile, and then shut the book on it for the time being while he put the gloves back on. Elijah in his dotage appeared to forgive him, or at least to sit with him and give him the No. 1 smile, and a whole era of unpleasantness seemed to drift away. "The country changed. I changed. I tried to mix boxing with religion, religion with boxing. It didn't work," he says. The new Ali comes in two parts. When writers ask about religion, he may say "I'm just

a fighter." Then again, if the mood is upon him, he may talk religion at length. As I get closer, I hear wildly different theories: that he is bored with the Muslims and that his mercurial self is ready to move on, if they don't object too violently; that he is bored with boxing and is deepening his knowledge of Islam.

All theories about Ali are true. I have just been to a press conference and trimmings at the UN, where he alternately stated that he would go on fighting for five years to help his black brothers and that his main goal is to quit as soon as possible. That's in the course of one hour.

This was my first step into Looking Glass Country, and it's a bewildering place. The comic characters were not there, Dundee and Bundini and the rest, but the master himself was, striding regally before his followers, his eyes darting round and seeing everything, but making only such contact as he chooses, like real royalty. There are foxes galore and brother Rachaman dressed to the nines and the ultimate Lewis Carroll character, Howard Cosell, making thunderous speeches to no one in particular. (I think he is dressing me down for something I wrote years ago, but his voice and his gaze are pitched at the East River, and he could be reading something into the Congressional Record.)

I shall follow Ali round the UN gardens and wherever he leads in the next section. But, meanwhile, the face in the glass has changed: fuller, heavier of course, than the young punk who looked like a World War II shavetail, but also more inward-looking, as if he has talked himself into a new position that he finds interesting. He comes back from exile looking as if he might even have lost his innocence.

Looking Glass Country

He looks more like a professional boxer than I expected. All those thousands of pictures do not quite convey the size or bunchiness of the neck and shoulders or the small precise steps. I remember the same sense of controlled grace when I met Gene Tunney in his retirement: they *are* like English policemen, goddamnit.

The face has been flattened ever so slightly by the hammers of Mars, and there is some reluctant scar tissue under the eyes. Yet he looks the better for it. Narcissus probably had a dull face without all those ripples on it—a few rounds with Frazier would have helped him too. Ali's eyes themselves are deadly weapons, black as carbon and jabbing in every direction, from impassive surroundings.

It is a solemn occasion and he is into his Sunday suit and his best behavior. He is giving some of his Wepner purse to Africare to irrigate the Sadat, and although the cause is life or death, you wouldn't guess it from the other speakers, who are drugged by the UN air and talk like leaflets. Ali is superb at showing boredom in repose: no twitching, no change of expression—just the essence of boredom captured indefinably as Olivier might capture it. If his future life is to consist of these semi-religious occasions, he will need ways to occupy his mind. Today, he settles for a ring magazine which he leafs through as the speakers drone.

When his own turn comes, he becomes moderately animated and he gives the only speech worth hearing. He has gone without breakfast today and feels the warning of real hunger—the first graphic remark of the day. He calls optimistically on the consciences of Ford and Kissinger. The talk is well prepared and carries a personal signature—rare in such speeches. "Wars on nations change maps. Wars on poverty map changes." He repeats the line carefully for the slow reporters. Well, OK, there is nothing wrong. But I feel deflated. After all I've written, I wonder if I haven't created something larger than life? He clearly puts on his pants one leg at a time.

Looking up I see faces—delegates, secretaries, international birds of passage—

"The once and future king"
posing for Sports Illustrated *cover, 1968.*

85

craning to look at him. He is larger than life for them too. The myth is real even if he isn't. He answers some questions in his most serious style (no, he will not be a Muslim leader, only a follower; yes, he has not trained enough for Wepner). Not a laugh in a carload. Then he shoulders his way out of the building and rumors start to fly immediately as to which way he is heading. It seems he is quite capable of slipping down a fire escape and leaving town, or of hanging around all day and addressing the General Assembly. Unpredictability is one of his most potent strategies: everybody is buzzing about him by now.

In the event he takes a stroll in the grounds, has a joshing exchange with Cosell of the minstrel show ("you callin' me a nigger?") variety and ducks back into the main building to bring Kurt Waldheim his greetings from Ali Nation. Only a few close aides are supposed to go with him, but the whole entourage tumbles in at Ali's behest, and the security guards shrug and give up.

Howard Cosell, prefight, 1972.

86

This gang can get past the doormen at Madison Square Garden, so ordinary humans haven't a chance.

At this point, your reporter is situated at the wrong end of the garden, having been faked out of his socks by the Master. ABC cameras have been set up down there, but this is no guarantee he'll show. No network is big enough to hold Ali to a schedule. To pass the time, Cosell introduces himself pleasantly to two security guards, who melt. Has no one any self-respect anymore? Not that Cosell isn't a nice fellow, in his strange way, but a security guard is supposed to be stuck on himself too. Isn't *any* citizen immune to *any* celebrity? Ho hum.

"I think he's coming." The rascal has got us all excited now. It is cold and windy, but Ali approaches with that majestic stillness, hands in pockets, moving only such parts as are necessary. He sits like a statue with Cosell: clearly (to answer that question) they are old friends and fellow troupers. Ali begins talking, and I get my first major surprise: he is almost inaudible. Even in his big shout scene, "Foreman must fall," the volume is no more than conversational. Otherwise, it is geared perfectly to the mike like a crooner's, so that it will sound big to the nation but no more than a whispered exchange to the bystanders.

He ends his little skit by pretending to beat up Cosell. With his back to the camera, he slaps his palm and grins. In fact, he grins a lot off camera, sheepishly, with an "ain't I a devil? isn't this just too much?" quality. As if he wants *us* to be in on the joke on *them:* the basic principle of dramatic irony, whether he knows it or not.

The cuffing of Cosell is also characteristic. When he is not still, he is most likely to be shadow boxing. He loves the motions

of punching and must throw thousands a day. Anyone old enough to walk can get Ali to square off. In fact, the first time I have seen him fight in the flesh is this very afternoon when two willowy foxes who have put on some gloves persuade him to mix it with them on the lawn. He manages to make it look like a real fight too and I'm beginning to think one of the foxes has a chance until she trips over her platform heel.

This is more like it. Ali was not himself in the UN. But now as he prances in the sun with two pretty girls, there is laughter and excitement in the bright cold air. His dour henchmen relax and the saturnine Rachaman smiles slyly. "You look tall," says the champ to the fox. "What are you, six feet?" "I'm five ten, but only when I'm lying down," answers the fox. Ali shakes his head in mock severity. Fie, for shame. He is scandalized by such talk. His flirting style reminds me of his hi-jinks at weigh-ins. Foreplay is everything.

The tribe moves off, with the King moving slowly in front and First Avenue, which is usually just another street, if that, suddenly fills with kids, mostly black, who've got wind of the Pied Piper's coming. I head for Ali's bus, but am cut off by a mob screaming variously, "I've got it" or "I haven't got it," alluding to the precious autograph, which must at least cure boils, like a saint's relic. My earlier disappointment has completely faded. Whether the crowd supplies the excitement or something in him, he is an Event all right.

I see him again later that afternoon in Neil Leifer's studio, and I learn that he does *not* necessarily like to have his picture taken. In fact, he seems to be having a tantrum. "I didn't want to come here." He enters pouting. "I didn't know I was coming here." Impossible to tell if he's really angry. Leifer, who's known him for years and has taken some of Ali's favorite pictures, proceeds rather tensely about his business.

Ali has brought his claque along, including the foxes, and as he plays to them, the original emotion becomes diffused, or mutates—I can't say precisely what the hell it does. He moans and rolls his head and even pretends to cry in his sitter's chair. The scenario calls for someone to throw water onto his oil-smeared face to produce that look of sweaty anguish which gives him a chance to take off his shirt, revealing little bands of fat on his ineffable torso, and also to break out a fresh routine. "Come on, white boy. You like that, don't you? You like wetting the nigger." He trails off. "Treating me like a nigger," he mumbles. All this for an audience of nine.

Meanwhile, though, he is doing a very professional job of posing. His face may not be the most mobile in the world, but it is totally at his command. "Sneer," "smile," the photographer has only to name the verb, and Ali's lip goes up or out the precise distance required. On the way out, he mutters to Leifer, "It's OK. I work hard at my job, you work hard at yours."

"Was he really angry?"

"I just don't know," admits Leifer.

If you can fool a good photographer, you must have your surfaces under pretty good control. And to go with this routine impenetrability, Ali has added a wanderlust that makes the butterfly as hard to pin outside the ring as in. For instance, having constructed a dream training camp in the Poconos, featuring Coretta's famous Kitchen, he is practically never there. As for his official residence in Cherry Hills,

New Jersey, it is the last place you expect to find him. Ralph Ellison has called him a wanderer, and it seems that the moment anything begins to look like a home, he pulls out.

Maybe this is because a home, like a past, would limit him and cramp his legend. Better to be Mr. Everyman and Mr. Noman, from everywhere and nowhere materializing suddenly like a good spirit and vanishing as quickly. Anyway that's how he seems to be training for chopped Chuck Wepner.

A week or so before the UN saga, I had laid plans to visit his training camp, on the solid grounds that since a) an out of shape fighter can look bad even against his sparring partners, and since b) talk has it that Ali has been hitting the jumbo malteds pretty hard, he has to stand still and train at some point. But I'm wrong. At the last moment, the reporters' bus is cancelled. Is he too fat to be seen? No, he's out of town someplace, preaching and doing good.

The next thing I know he's in Houston accepting awards, giving away awards, carrying on. Then suddenly, he's passing through his camp on the way to the UN, where he announces that he's really going to get down to it now for the remaining three weeks (he's only got two). He checks out an old fight film of Wepner's in about ten minutes flat, makes faces for Leifer and heads back to work.

Or so it seems. But by now Ali moves so fast he even outruns his own people, and no one seems to know for sure where he is. I am about to head for the Poconos one more time when word arrives that he has broken camp for good. What, where? Rumors of his comings and goings suddenly rival Patty Hearst's. His promoters say he's

in Cleveland, and the Times says he's in New York, sparring at the Felt Forum, but he hasn't been seen at either place. It is a game he plays with the world: dancing out of range, then suddenly sticking out his face and pulling it back again.

Is there a practical reason, or is it just a blind assertion of freedom, like a teenager's? This, mind you, is eleven days before a championship fight, and all that's known for sure is that Ali left camp in his super house-bus in the putative direction of Cleveland. Maybe he's training away his flab in secret. Maybe anything. A woman reporter comforts me. "Rock stars are worse," she says. That is the context I see him in right now—a star at large, go-man-going to no place in particular.

I gather that the above is downright sedentary compared with his schedule when he's *not* in training. Ali craves motion (although he used to have drastic plane fright) and during his exile he had to keep going even though there was no place to go, like a retired businessman starting for the office. Travel is his magic charm against the demons of boredom. He likes to collect cars and drives them like a beatnik on the road to nowhere.

Meanwhile, his elusiveness is abetted by one of the cagiest inner circles since Cardinal Richelieu. Anyone can see him publicly—I think it is his secret wish to be seen by every man, woman and child on the planet earth—but to see him privately is harder than getting a visa from the Chinese Embassy. Ah these Capricorns. Perhaps there is something to that stuff after all. Ali prefers a million people to one, and so did Mr. Nixon. I look it up in the Book of Nonsense, and it says that for Capricorns, the desk is the man, the medals are the

89

At contract signing with Chuvalo, top; Frazier, bottom.

ates with writers. Right now he is fantasizing a full-length fight with the ill-starred Wepner, including dialogue. "Show me something, boy. You're nothin' but a sissy," whup whup. The table bounces seismically as he straightens from his crouch. "Call me a nigger." Whup whup. He plays Wepner's part too. "I want that championship so bad (puff) I wanna get out of the liquor business (puff)." So Ali whups him again and nicks me in the elbow with his backswing—which is fast and full, giving him plenty of leverage for the next phantom punch six inches to my left. His shoulders are moving like pistons and his seated legs flail. If Ali had to fight sitting down, he would still sting like a bee.

He is fully at home now, in a dressing room full of newsmen, and I am free to judge how artificial his UN performance was—and by extension other non-boxing performances. This is the Real Act, as opposed to the phony real act. Sportswriters are his earliest partners in Ali Industries and there is a businesslike rapport between them that doesn't always show up in print.

Since these affairs are among the three or four basic rituals of image maintenance, and since they seem to be as stylized as Japanese No plays, a quick flip through of this one will convey the rest. I have since been to a dozen and they vary as little as the Catholic mass. Picture Ali sitting center-stage preoccupied, glancing at a newspaper; this is a prop since he does indeed read with difficulty. It suggests that the questioners are interrupting him, and he returns to it occasionally to show what's important around here. It will be discarded as he loosens up. Every shy kid knows the procedure.

The reporters clustered round range

soldier. They are defined by their trimmings, whether by guards in pretty uniforms or by championship belts. I know this is absurd because I'm a Capricorn myself. A telegram appears in *Publisher's Weekly*, signed by the man himself boasting about his own autobiography *(The Greatest,* what else?) and saying he isn't going to cooperate with any other book writer.

The next thing I know, I am settling next to him on a training table in Cleveland three days before his next fight, and he is throwing hooks and jabs that make the table bounce and my tail sore. Asking Ali not to cooperate with a writer is to defy nature, as whoever signs his telegrams must know. Every time he breathes, he cooper-

92

from rock-culture kids to gym-smart vets, and there is no question the vets get the better, more relevant answers. Otherwise, he tends to talk about what he wants to talk about, in a curious mixture of guile and free-association. To begin with, someone pops him a question about his new house in Chicago, which gets him off on his second favorite topic, bricks and mortar. After describing the joint from frame to portcullis, he moves into town planning—specifically a mosque-cum-shopping center that he has in mind for Cleveland and another for Atlanta. No one can remember by now who brought this subject up, or why, but he plays his vision out anyway, of shiny shop windows and glistening beauty parlors and a spiffy all-black restaurant that sounds too pretty to eat in, before we can get down to business.

This turns out to be perfunctory, Chuck Wepner being what he is. The sales pitch for this fiasco is that Ali is out of shape. So he says his ribs are sore, and he touches first the left and then the right to verify this. Also he has a cold (the sneezes sound genuine) and he is overweight. By hunching over, he can produce small rungs in his stomach, which he pinches mournfully. By now, we are convinced he is in spanking condition. Vic Ziegel of the *New York Post* sums it up. "Ali, you're a real mess," he says.

One senses that out-of-shapeness will serve to sell more than one fight from now on and will become part of the Routine. Hence the following glazed mumble: "Someone's gonna get me . . . I'm just hanging on . . . tired . . . no more glory . . . just fighting for bricks. I've done miracles already. (He lists miracles, with voice rising.)" It needs work, but in five years he'll have it cold.

The other tentative pitch *du jour* is that Wepner is a dirty fighter. Dundee claims he has seen the Bleeding One practice deadly combinations of kidney and rabbit punches, topped off with a vicious blow to the top of the head called a Wepner whopper. "Do you serve that with a sesame roll?" asks Dick Young of the *New York Daily News*. Such is the atmosphere of a minor fight: goofier and more revealing than the major ones. Ali has nothing to concentrate on but his acting, and in helping the press to create stories out of nothing.

Wepner's unrelieved swinishness is Ali's cue to return to dreamland. Supposing Wepner does do those awful things—"well, I'm going to take the law into my hands. I'm going to tackle him around the legs, and I'm going to stomp him and bite him." The filthiest fight in history is quickly conjured up, culminating with a vision of Ali's title being taken away again for foul play. This, in turn, will lead to mass rioting and bloodshed in the streets, if not World War III itself; but after all that settles down, he will gamely hit the comeback trail again, and his second resurrection will be even more glorious than his first, to be held in some celestial stadium yet to be built and packed to the sky.

Right now, he can think of no new stories to tell about himself, so he tells the same one over and over again, adjusting it to the various Wepners as they come and go. He has to devise a way of losing his title so he can make another comeback and yet another. What else is there to do? Against Wepner's dirtiness, escalating foul play seems to be the best route to disgrace; against another fighter, he would have to think of something else. "*Any*thing I do in the ring can get the temper of the nation racing," he says, conjuring wild visions of unspeakable acts that will get him barred once more. "Controversy is my middle name."

He stretches, takes off his sweat-socks. The dramatist has finished his workout. Is this the new, tested-in-the-furnace Ali, or the hambone as before? When he is hawking tickets, he seems just about the same. But other themes crop up obsessively between the cracks and I'll just lay them on the table like someone emptying his pockets. Will he go into politics? "Not your kind of politics." What other kind is there? Well, some manner of travelling, preaching with a friend of his who is "ten times as good as Malcolm X ever was." (The slur on his old Master is casual, blood-curdling.) How about Herbert Muhammad? "He is the wisest. In all these years he's only visited the gym twice." This separation of church and sport means that Ali is free as a bird to swoop down "and catch everything that's happening."

The talk turns domestic. His wife and children are in town, so Ali the husband plays a number on that. He tells about sleeping with his two-year-old son, Muhammad Ibn Ali, last night, and I can only say the story is no duller than most such. It ends with the kid going pee pee, but my notes are unclear as to how we reached that point. Ali then works up a routine about the horrors of taking kids out, about how they spill food on their clothes and don't fasten them right in the restroom. His fascination with objects is evident; most people would add something about the noise and aggravation of children, but Ali only minds the shirt sticking out and the mess that lands on it. Soup, orange juice—Ali grimaces as

it all rains down on Junior.

The moral is that only women with their special gifts are fit to cope with such squalor. ("I'm not your mommy" he tells his son at the height of the pee pee story.) This leads into a eulogy of Muslim women and their high moral standards, and a special plug for his daughter, Maryum, who already speaks Arabic and is destined to be a strong independent woman who takes no lip from him. All this while he is flirting idly with a passing fox—another one of his props these days. He adds that all his children are taught to pray five times a day and refrain from pork and will go to an Islamic University in Chicago.

What's interesting is that he gets all this into a boxing interview with veteran sportswriters who barely bother to take it down. He is an ordained minister, and don't you forget it. His cloth kept him out of the draft, and he isn't abandoning it now. Apropos of this, I learn something interesting from Dick Schaap. The night Ali impressed me so much by dressing down Joe Namath, he said afterwards, "You know I have to do that stuff. The CIA is watching, the FBI is watching. . . ."

The Ali who suddenly plunks himself next to me is not the solemn preacher, but an amiable boyish fellow with a shy smile, not all that far removed from the kid who came busting out of Louisville strutting and laughing. Is there really a thundering holy man inside this kid? Or is being holy just a duty like facing East from time to time?

I get some kind of an answer before I leave Cleveland—in fact, at least two kinds. But in the meantime, more of the Ali Players have checked in. Angelo Dundee is the very model of a fight trainer in a boxing comedy. He bounces in, shooting

94

wisecracks and explanations from both hips, yet all business. He is gentle for a fight trainer, and has needed to be to ride out the Black Power period; someone tells me he has a Chinese personality and can adapt to anything, even Ali. One look at his face tells me he will be a source of cigars. (No one smokes around Ali—but Angelo without a cigar is like a chipped sculpture.) He tells me how he trained lizards to do push-ups in Zaire, propping up one foot with a pebble, but says he couldn't teach Australian koalas a damn thing.

Drew Bundini Brown enters and perches in his clown's nest. He will have to be funny, the world's most gruesome burden. If the years are hard on heavy-weights, they are murder on court jesters. To the untutored ear, Bundini sounds like a vaudevillian who's forcing it with stale material. But it's hard to tell, with his jungle-bird voice, exactly what he's saying. Several less celebrated wits, such as Walter Youngblood, the only Muslim left in Ali's fight corner, and Gene Kilroy of the white persuasion, are getting off some pretty good lines without even trying. Of all titles, Bundini's is the hardest to hold onto.

It's a cheerful dressing room, as advertised. The jokes are averagely bawdy. As Ali lays stretched on the rubbing table, there is some speculation as to how much a centerfold in *Playgirl* would fetch. He has a Brigitte Bardot way of flipping his little towel around that might fetch something. One of the lesser wags suggests that with that curvaceous rump, Ali would have had to learn to fight in jail; either that, or come out (a swish imitation completes the sentence). No response from Ali, who is sleepily receiving a rubdown that relaxes you just to watch, from the witchcraft fingers of his Cuban masseur. The locker room is his real home, whether it's a streamlined number like this one or the back of a bus in Daytona, and the rubbing table is his bed. Luis Sarria, the masseur, is definitely part of the cast. He doesn't speak English and he doesn't exactly gabble in Spanish, and in repose, which is nearly always, he could pass for a wood carving of a slave on a plantation. Yet he proves to be a man of exquisite alertness, who has the lighter out before you've reached for the cigarette, and who makes a very warm friend. (I know because I had a silent lunch with him.) With the cunning of drift, Ali has chosen the finest corner in boxing. Frazier once accused him of having too many white men in it. But boxing is too serious to be messed up by racism.

Outside the dressing room Ali's men may seem wary and aloof, as if they were perpetually escorting him through dangerous crowds. But here locked away from the world, they are a cozy family. There is no discernible black-white friction: Dundee swaps gags and memories with Bundini, and Kilroy says, "I hear the circus came to town. Us."

At some point, I am introduced to Ali, and he asks if I am the guy who wrote something nice about him that morning. No mistake, his attitude changes when he hears you're a writer. His respect is immediate. Less so brother Rachaman's, whose principal occupation seems to be glowering at white men, and who asks me sharply how I'm getting all this down. A writer without a pad or a tape recorder is obviously up to no good. Nervously I yank out my notebook. I feel frisked.

For the next few days, Ali rambles the streets of Cleveland, visiting schools and hospitals at random or just plain visiting. He prides himself on his accessibility, but that is too mild a term: he could declare himself a throughway. After roadwork, he is likely to mosey into the coffee shop and rap with whomever fate sends him. His attention is like some electronic device that comes in strongly, then fades without warning. The only rule I could figure was that when you want it you can't get it, and that when you've given up he may suddenly start talking. It's his way of controlling the scene.

It also means that he can fall back on prepared material—of which there is now so much that he can appear to ad lib for hours. Certain oldies and goodies recur everyday. "If he even dream he can beat me, he should wake up and apologize." "I'm so fast I can turn out the light and be in bed before it's dark." "I can hospitalize a brick." His entourage can reel off Ali quotes all day long. It is a bit like the Walt Disney studios. Who knows where the quotes came from originally? Dundee helps with the poems ("I'm pretty good at rhymes"). Another was written by a German journalist called Erik Ells and yet another was allegedly stolen from a student. "Don't boast, it was lousy," Ali told the kid—but did he even say that? Dundee and the boys puff along like Santa's workmen, and it all comes out under Ali's imprint.

How intelligent is Ali himself? Estimates veer confidently between near-moron and genius, and the surprising thing is that he gives both impressions at once. When he bombed out on the Army IQ test, a lot of people thought he did it intentionally—but no one was sure. I'm not sure as I listen today, but I'll keep working on it.

Meanwhile the hoopla, which is his real business (fighting Wepner is just an incident) continues, like a kid beating a tin can. Ali tells the press the next day that he weighs 239 pounds and is growing by the moment. In fact, he weighs 225 and is shrinking. So he tells us all the things he plans to eat in the next two days to blow himself up, a veritable Howard Johnson's dessert menu—another of his famous lists of objects. He seems to think in lists. And he certainly likes his food: no wheezing glutton ever made peach cobbler sound so desirable.

The weight joke is wearing thin, so he swings into a list of celebrities who are less accessible than he is—Namath, Sinatra, etc.—after that, a list of countries that are in his corner, including (and he drops this in quite casually) the Palestine guerillas.

This is one of those ominous notes that the new Ali sounds from time to time. Yet it all seems quite innocent in the sunny locker room, as Sarria kneads his gleaming flesh and Ali spitballs, "Man who fights me is challenging God himself. Because I'm

97

fighting for a cause. There's something else in the ring with me. The rise of the black people. I don't have to train because of Allah." Yeah, sure, Ali. Black Power, Allah, peach cobbler—it's all incorporated into the routine by now, and nobody pays it any mind.

Yet before the week is out, the Muslim note will come out more than once, bitter and humorless, as the dark brooding side of his personality struggles for control of laughing boy. Today laughing boy wins out easily. Ali wrestles an English journalist, a fat jolly chap with a mustache who chortles with delight, and he ends the session rehearsing his "You are *doomed*" shtik for tomorrow's weigh-in. "Don't laugh," says an assistant, but Ali can't help it. He points menacingly. "You are doomed," he says and cracks up completely.

Or is even the laugh rehearsed?

I am right about Dundee's cigars. They are excellent. I bum a ride with him back to the hotel and he tells me how he taught Ali to cooperate with writers—which is a bit like teaching Niagara how to fall. It seems, though, that Young Cassius used to cooperate with everyone he met indiscriminately, not realizing there was anything special about writers. He certainly knows now, referring to our motley little crew as "the world's greatest" whenever he spots us.

Dundee himself is a curious figure to find in back of the Promotion Machine. He loves publicity yet is a comfortable, homey man who'll kill a valuable hour talking fishing; he jokes with writers all day and plays poker with them all night, yet does not leave you with that slimy feeling on your hands that you frequently get from P.R. people; he has earned a fortune for

Ali with his rhymes and gimmicks, yet for a long time took very little for himself. He is also a kind of all-purpose relative that they don't have a name for, which comes in handy for the many roles of Ali. Lord Ali can tell him, "get me a Coke, white boy," and he'll go get it; or little orphan Ali can say, "where's Angie? I need Angie" and he'll be there. His life is boxing, and so long as he has a good boy in the ring, he doesn't care how he does it.

To Angie, Ali hasn't changed a day since they met: he is fixed for eternity as a fun-loving, irrepressible kid, and Dundee doesn't want to talk about the rest. The Muslims have left him alone, he says, and he has certainly left them alone. It's the only thing to do with Muslims. Ever since Ali came strutting into Dundee's gym, demanding the best trainer in the business, he has had charge of Ali the Lovable. Ali acknowledges the debt. "Angie has the connections and the right complexion." As a fight draws closer Ali seems to depend more on Dundee, calling for him from the rubbing table. After the fight they will drift apart again. I get a sudden feeling that when Dundee leaves for good, Laughing Boy will die.

Too severe. Yet there is a palpable change in atmosphere when Dundee and Kilroy leave the dressing room. Ali is as susceptible as a voodoo initiate to the spirits around him and in the presence of a blithe fellow like Angie, his heart lifts. But I wouldn't be sure of him in a roomful of hate.

That night, I close the bar with Ali's father, which is not hard to do in Cleveland. Mr. Clay is indeed full of the old St. Nick. He's a handsome devil with a mean sparkle in his eye that could lead to all kinds of crazy mischief. He also shares his son's "ain't that something" grin; in action their faces are more alike than I had supposed. Mr. Clay is reputed to be a ladies' man, and he certainly looks it. Tonight, though, he wants to talk about painting.

It seems he is self-taught, and he likes to spread the word. The toughest thing to master is perspective in color; then the tints and highlights that are not the color you think they are. "A fall green isn't really green—it's yellow." Likewise the foam on his beer isn't really white, and neither is the saucer next to it. Other painters? Well, Norman Rockwell is pretty good, "but he's not an all the way round artist." He peers at me, and notices a bluish tint in my cheek, not surprising at that time of night; but he says that he would concentrate on a point in my forehead "if Ise painting you."

He is animated, urgent. Surely he was a good teacher for his boys—or was he too much for them? He says they both helped out with the sign painting and showed some talent. But when I asked him what he'd expected Cassius (he still calls him that) to be someday, he surprised me by saying "an attorney."

I am still puzzled by Ali's relative illiteracy, coming from such a bright, didactic daddy. So I ask Mr. Clay about poetry and such, and he recites the words of a couple of popular songs with considerable feeling. The lights are flickering and one hates to take notes in such pleasant company, and for the life of me I can't remember what they were. But when he had done, he said, "Gives you something to think about, doesn't it?"

Before putting my notebook away to carouse in earnest, I had jotted down a couple of other things about Mr. Clay. He

is still an ambitious man and plans to put on an exhibit of paintings in Louisville. He is bitter about the years he wasted working for a living, and says more than once that an artist needs independence—an echo of Ali's crowing "I am free." It is easy to believe that Mr. Clay periodically might have added the white man to his list of grievances: a black artist doesn't have much of a chance in hell. But he is a defiant man and will put the name Cassius Clay back on the map somehow. It is no problem guessing where Ali got his hang-up on fame, and on names.

I stress Mr. Clay's optimism because of something else he said. It seems that since Ali got rich "I can't get no work. Everyone says 'you don't need no money'." I have no way of judging the truth of this, only the bitterness. "Cassius' success destroyed me," he says. And then, with a baleful glare, "Don't ever let them get bigger than you." But how do you stop them? How do you even think about it? Mr. Clay's good nature is burned away, leaving a hot coal of rage.

When I saw Mr. Clay the next day, he said, "What did I say to you last night?"

"You talked about the color green."

"Oh."

He looked bored.

As for Mrs. Clay, she sits in the lobby a lot with her friends and kin who travel to Ali's fights in a body, out to the third and fourth cousin. Ali may not have a home but he carries his old one with him and it reassembles for his fights. Odessa is a natural porch sitter with a high little girl voice and the patience of an anchorite. If she moves once every ten minutes, it's a busy afternoon. Yet her eyes look around brightly to pick up acquaintances, whom she greets with unflagging warmth.

There seems no point interviewing her, because she has been giving the same interview for 12 years. Right now, someone is playing one back to her on a tape recorder, and she beams at her own sing-song answers. Cassius (she calls him that too) was always a nice boy, he's always thinking about others, she is confident he'll win tonight. Odessa is impenetrably sweet, and one feels she has held a volcanic family together by sheer good will.

Listening to her, one's mind begins to rock and it is suddenly a long summer afternoon in Louisville, with friends dropping in and out for "two cups of love," to quote one of Ali's poems. "You all be careful and don't get hurt, my baby," she once told Cassius on the way into the ring. Today the talk is mostly down-home gossip plus plans for the evening. She is worried about getting ready in plenty of time, and brings this up periodically. She laughs a lot, but mostly out of good nature, not because of anything funny. She is a nice woman, and I don't feel too bad about eavesdropping: the Clays share their daily lives with anyone who'll listen. Their real secrets they don't even tell each other, I suspect.

On the last day, I see the two Clays together for the first time. It is nice to see them life-size and not as the parents of Apollo. It seems Odessa used to know the Clays way back when—they used to meet in Aunt Coretta's Kitchen, long before Odessa married Cassius, Sr. Ali comes from a tribe as well as a family: a tribe of loving hard-working people who keep an eye on each other. Mr. Clay looks a little awkward in this Baptist Lady setting, but polite and obliging. One is reminded of how tough any life is to get through, let alone when you're black and not quite talented enough;

and I feel these two have done pretty damn well. They are as different from each other as earth and fire, but they combine strangely in their son, who takes turns being now the one, now the other, even in his press conferences.

Speaking of which, the hoopla peaks as good hoopla should the day before the fight. The lobby of the Marriott Hotel crawls with pimps and whores, or facsimile pimps and whores (everyone falls into a role at fight-time, and I am now a facsimile sportswriter, low-minded and unkempt). Promoters and press agents jostle and gouge as they did in Tex Rickard's day, while preliminary boys discuss obscure dates in out of the way clubs. The fight crowd moves on like a gypsy caravan barely touching reality at any point and hence, almost changeless. It is the most exciting scene left in American life and makes a political convention look like a rag and bone sale.

This is Ali's scene, says Dr. Ferdie Pacheco, at the gym the next day. For all his religious conversion, it is exciting to be around so much crazy sin. And long after his body had begun to resist training and his spirit refuses to concentrate, he will still crave this part: floating around the ring jabbing and feinting, while the dudes chatter and the foxes stare meltingly. If time could stop now, Ali would be in heaven. It's always the same and always different. A small boy touted as a karate champion pops into the ring and tries to take him on, with a few playful kicks. Then Redd Foxx, the comedian, is up there, sparring with Ali, as everyone spars with Ali. Foxx: "You ever hit a gun?" That kind of stuff. Hog heaven, for a man who once worshipped celebrities himself and fought for their autographs. James Brown, the singer,

checks in and my goodness, it's Mr. Billy Eckstine.

We are down in the dressing room again, Ali's rumpus room, and Ali is carolling the praises of James Brown. "He's everywhere, like me," he locates Brown's importance on the Ali spectrum. "We're both Gods in Ethiopia." To think is to act, so Ali does a zany imitation of Brown, skittering his legs and moaning. More an imitation of Ali than of Brown.

After that, Foxx and Eckstine fall to it, swapping the stories that once had the Apollo Theatre in a roar. The reporters are getting a $50 night club show for nothing, but that's just one of their normal burdens. Ali sits slumped against the wall in his terry cloth robe, happy as a schoolboy while the *famous men* perform for him. A couple of the jokes have to be explained to him and he doesn't hesitate to ask. In this sense, he is curiously honest.

When his own turn comes, he follows a string of shit stories with a manure story ("I can't use them words"), and for once he seems inhibited and actually stammers in front of these professional comics. He is, though he says so himself, a humble man: it is one of the weird secrets of his success. Once you notice it, his wildest boasts never bother you again.

The manure story is well chosen—harmless enough to protect his image, naughty enough to keep him from looking prudish. It's about a bird whose wings freeze and he lands in some shit which thaws his wings and—well it isn't worth going on with. You'll find it in *1001 Gags* or on some risqué cocktail napkin. What's interesting is that it is a fable rather than a joke-joke. Ali is much given to parables, and even when he does his "heavy think-

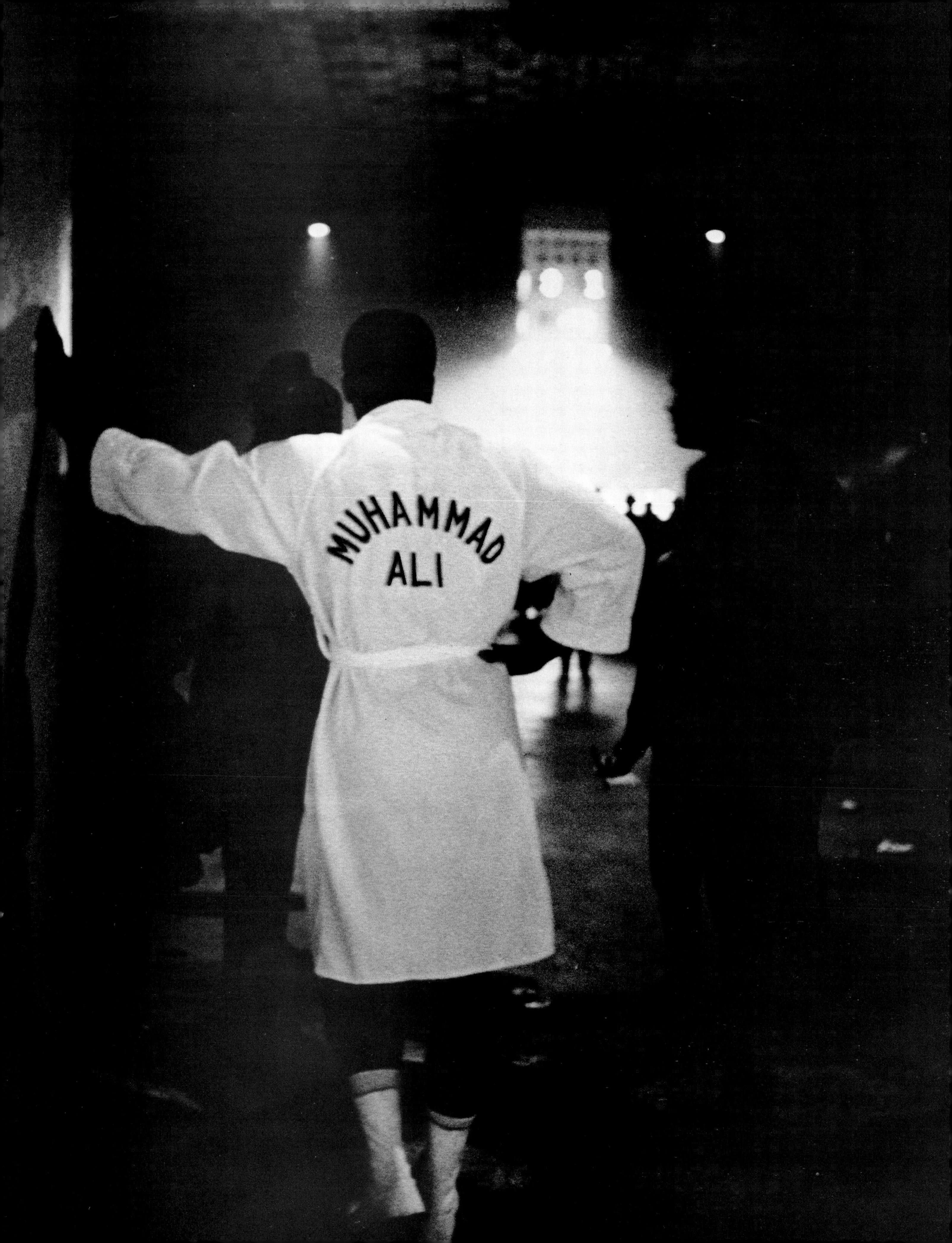
MUHAMMAD
ALI

ing," he does it in stories.

"Redd Foxx, Billy Eckstine, Lloyd Price," he caressingly lists the names. "With all this soul in my corner, how can I lose?" The fun is reaching its apex. Bundini is holding his own court on the training table and Foxx goes over for an exchange of ribaldries. This is no time to snub the house jester. Everything is geared now for the big banana, the weigh-in. Ali the media freak has his climax tonight; the fighter has his tomorrow. They are on slightly different schedules. Right now, no one can even remember who he's fighting.

The weigh-in is the usual hysterical mess. "It's hard to be humble when you're so great." Ali the clown has reached the end of the line; there is nothing he can do that he hasn't done before. Only the dark side of Ali can continue.

Hence the only original note at the Cleveland Coliseum weigh-in. For the first time, he uses the phrase "he called me a nigger" on the airwaves. It is a joke of course. Ali uses the word nigger more than all his detractors put together, and he has

reduced the word "nigger" to such absurdity that no one can ever use it seriously again.

Yet it isn't very funny. It doesn't come from the wellspring of Nonsense where Ali usually gets his jokes, but from a mixed neighborhood where jokes turn easily to snarls and blows. Earlier in the week, he has given his first public anti-Christian speech. Could Elijah's death be bringing him out of the mosque? And the next night against Wepner, there will be just a pinch more racism than usual and it will be just a little less funny. But before going into this and kindred matters, I propose stepping outside the glass to look at his career from the time of his return from Limbo, when America graciously agreed to get off his back, till now, to see why the trajectory of his celebrity has moved him inevitably in the shadow direction and may move him further.

Meanwhile though, the old Ali, the man-child, is still hanging in there, kicking his legs on the training table. Angelo Dundee is telling us that *our* Evil Eye, a chap called Finkel, is cleaner and better looking than *their* Evil Eye. Finkel ended World War II by putting his hex in a bottle. This time he's mailing it in. The white magic of fight trainers chases black magic away. The great Cuban welterweight Kid Gavilan is being kidded for his lack of English. "Sugar Ray taught him all he know. 'Don't hit me no more'." "Hey, boy!" says someone. "Did you say Roy?" is the answer. This is almost the camp password. Even the stern faces of his Muslim assistants crack in smiles. There is nothing wrong in Wonderland, and not a cloud in the sky.

For now. Everything about Ali is for now.

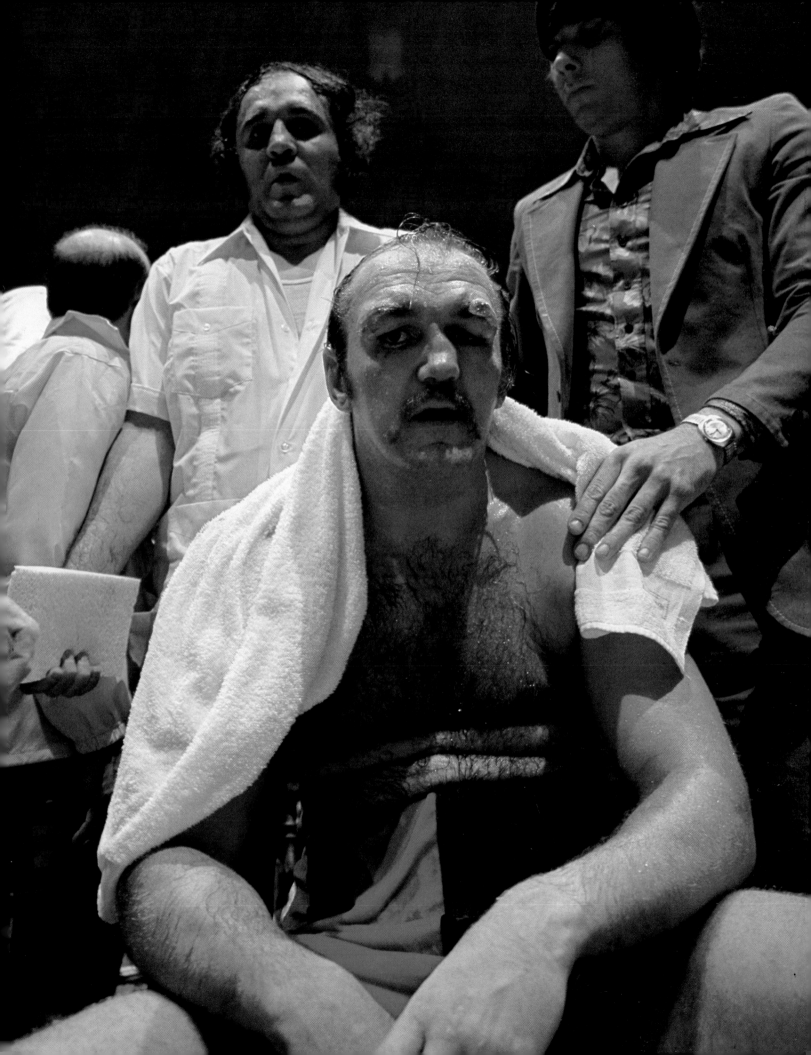

The Road to Mecca

Ali was actually turned down by the Army before the Army was turned down by him. He scored 78 on the IQ test, which was considered too low even for cannon fodder, and he was registered a phantom 1-Y. How much such little humiliations bother Ali is impossible to say, because he never shows pain. He had finished 358 in a class of 371 at Louisville High, but this is now considered a joke on the high school; and this latest failure was considered a joke on IQ tests.

But, considering Ali's obsession with intelligence, one wonders whether he really likes having his nose rubbed in his inadequacies like this. Maybe the story of his draft resistance begins here and not with the Muslim rationale. Later on, in its ravening lust for bodies to count, the Army lowered its standards; but nobody wants to join a club on those terms. The white establishment had already published to the world, "Ali is dumb"; all his verbal fakes and feints are a trick. The black boy hasn't got it up here.

Coming hot from his Muslim conversion, this may have confirmed him in his feeling that white man's intelligence is devil's intelligence, and that there is a better and different kind of wisdom outside of IQ. So he steeped himself in the sting and float sayings of Bundini and the wild insights of Elijah. "Black men put the moon up 66 million years ago . . . they drilled into the earth and with high explosives caused a piece to go into space . . . if anybody lands on it, his eyes will pop out or sumpt'n." Try putting that in an IQ test.

The actual draft rejection was as routine as most such bureaucratic happenings, except for the popping flashbulbs and the press conference afterwards, which made it instant history, the first tableau of exile. It must have been a tense scene, with so many cultural cross-currents at play: the white-sheriff scene slamming against the celebrity mystique, and the black and peace power out in the streets.

Ali was quieter that day than he ever was in the ring. At his side was a white

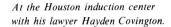

*At the Houston induction center
with his lawyer Hayden Covington.*

lawyer, and outside a supporting army of
white war resisters, but it was ultimately
a black decision and Ali plunged right afterwards deeper into Islam than he had ever
been. Every question now was fielded by
a Muslim answer: Allah's behind me, Elijah's behind me—better be *someone* behind
me.

Meanwhile Islam, for all its aloofness,
was being swept along in the larger torrent
of Black Power. Burn baby burn. "Watts,
Detroit—your city will be next." It wasn't
easy for the friendly Ali to adopt the man-
nerisms: truculence, menace, contempt. But
for a short while, white reporters found him
at least cool and impersonal and more ob-
trusively black than he'd ever been. He had
to: his whole union was doing it, and he'd
never had a union before.

"I'm standing up for my people even
if I have to go to jail," he said. He couldn't
have held out for three years without Islam
and the race issue to bolster him; and however much his quick-change soul may want
to move on from that now, they are still
there demanding their dues.

Which is not to say the exile was spent
in monastic gloom. Ali isn't ready for that.
Controlling his melancholy is one of his
greatest disciplines, and after a suitable
period of mourning, he hit the lecture circuit with a bang, revelling in a new kind
of heroism: the $1,500 a night martyr, daz-
zling the white college kids with something
other than boxing. It was his first big step
outside the sports pages, and there is no
evidence that he strained every nerve to get
back in. After some laughable attempts had
been made to promote fights behind the
American Legion's back (each time

thwarted by timid politicians), Ali simply gave up looking. A black who knows him well says that he was less bitter than anyone during his suspension. And in 1969 he was saying, "I don't anger toward the commissioners or the American Legion or the Foreign Legion [*sic*] . . . nobody ever heard me protest about losin' in anything." The furor around Ali was now ten times as big as he was, and he enjoyed sitting in the middle, watching.

By 1970, Black Power had about reached the end of the line in frightening white people for profit and by now the gun was in the other hand. Fred Hampton was dead, along with Ali's great fan Martin Luther King; Huey Newton was in jail and Bobby Seale was up on a murder rap. So a certain mellowing was only good sense. A rather subdued Ali, minus boasts and poems, began to have his comeback prepared for him. With the strenuous help of a black state senator called Leroy Johnson, he fought some unpublicized exhibitions in Atlanta for $5 top, and when the Georgia sky didn't fall in on him, plans were made for a real fight in Atlanta against Jerry Quarry, the Great White Hopeless: with nothing hanging over it but a few paunchy pickets and Governor Maddox's undying curse.

All heavyweights have mysteriously large entourages, but when he hit Atlanta for the Quarry fight, Ali seemed to have a whole religion on his back. Whether or not he pays the full Muslim tithe, which is a whopper, his handouts to individual Muslims and pseudo-Muslims would fill a stadium, and they just about did that night. Ali waved a batch of them on in past the bemused ticket-takers. He is a leader now and will take care of his people.

And along with the boys in black came a glittering array of men's mink hats and beaded maxicoats and all the spangles and see-throughs that the Muslims are dedicated to stamping out. Ali's following has swelled to include every dude with a dream and every slit-to-the-navel fox, plus the cream of the black celebrity register—Julian, Coretta, the Reverend Jesse. The young minister has returned from the desert to quite a hoedown, and judging from Cleveland, he doesn't want it to ever end.

But getting back to business, alas. He has crystallized as a symbol, but he has slipped a bit as a fighter. Knocking out Quarry is the least he can do, and he does it, but without the old grace notes. A new pattern has emerged. The occasion is everything, and belongs on the fashion pages; the fight is just a fight. Next he knocks out the bumbling Oscar Bonavena in 15 rounds, settling very little. Bonavena is the kind of ox-like fighter that often makes Ali look bad, as if his clumsiness were catching. Neither fight could account for the incredible tension that had already begun building for his first championship fight with Joe Frazier.

The interest in that one comfortably soars above boxing. People who never saw a fight, those who hate violence and those who wallow in it, all had violent opinions—as if political passion could make one an expert for a night. The atmosphere was more like that of a presidential election than a prize fight, with barbershops rent in two and voices raised under hair driers.

It's true that nobody wanted much part

113

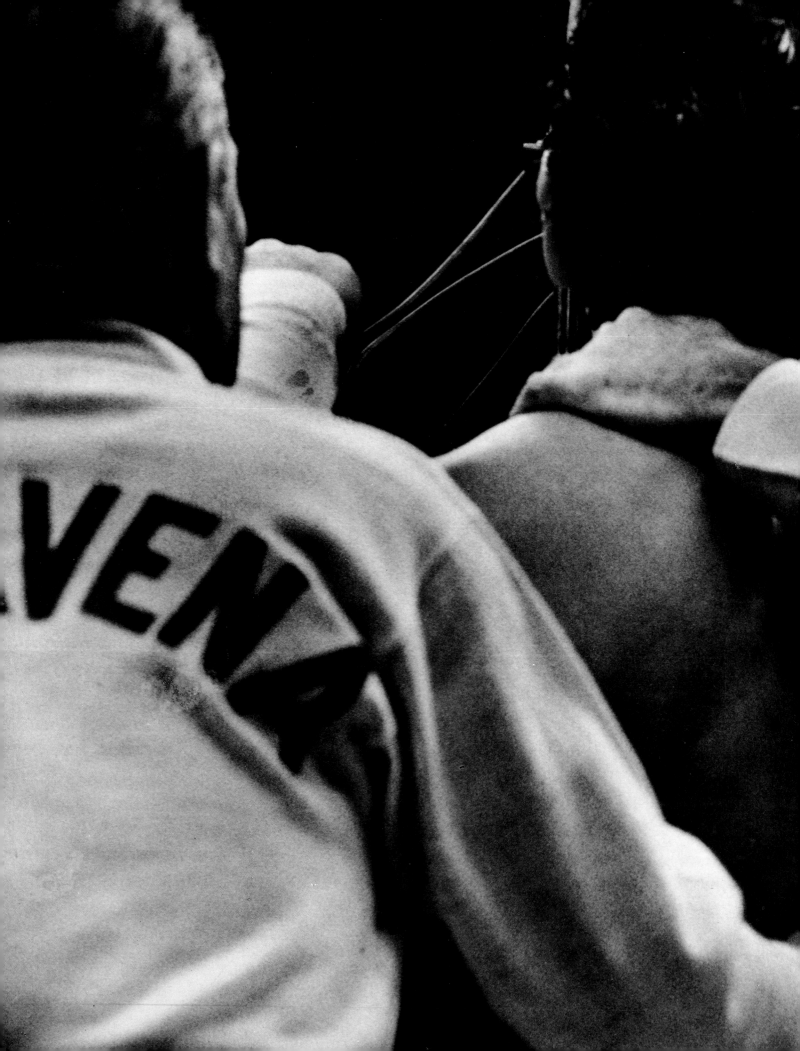

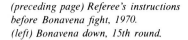
of Vietnam by then, but draft resisters were still marooned in Canada or a fate worse than Canada, and here was the baddest of them all lining up a seven figure payday in the States. In the twisted shadow of that malformed war, many things got distorted. And Ali's old carnival act suddenly seemed malignant and sinister to one bunch, inspired and revolutionary to another. It might be the same old act, but history had enlarged it.

Trust Ali to rise to an occasion. He had exchanged some racist claptrap with Quarry and Bonavena, but this was barely worthy of early century "Mr. Bones" talk. (Bonavena called him "a black kangaroo," which is almost an endearment.) But these were just tune-ups; even the Act needs work. For Frazier, he pumped up some of his best material; under pressure the Act got better and more complicated.

Which is ironical, because he didn't even *need* the Act this time. Looking back, there is something almost bathetic about Ali still trying to make enemies when he had so many real ones. The hawks out there wanted him killed; and here he was with his old Gorgeous George patter, trying to annoy them still further. The goofy self-promotion of a more innocent time became a symbol like Viet Cong flags and hardhats—or the piffling radio talks of P.G. Wodehouse in World War II that were denounced in the House of Commons. But this would have been the event of his life if he'd trained in a Buddhist monastery.

It is an interesting footnote to the history of hustle that this overreaction was exactly what Ali's act needed. As noted, Ali is not a natural comic, and left to their own

117

devices, his boasts and prophecies would have gone the way of Twiggy. But with a little Black Muslim menace added, and some red-neck rage, the act was reborn. It did suit his face now, as pure comedy had not. His features were ideal for mixing light comedy and his own anger in an equilibrium so fine that even a fellow con man like Cosell couldn't always tell which was which; and the audience experienced a totally new emotion between fear and laughter. It was like a real gun going off on stage. The actor becomes more than an actor. Vietnam had made Ali the Myth come true.

One more flourish before he gets in the ring with Frazier. He appoints himself once again the Black Man—and makes it stick. He has tried it before against Terrell and Patterson, but their colors didn't change before our eyes. This time, as in some Genêt play, Ali makes us see Color as *purely* a state of mind. He appoints Frazier white for a night, and presto, Frazier becomes one of us. Again, credit the Houston draft board: he has behaved blackly, Frazier whitely, so Frazier becomes the latest great white hope and their combined fortunes are ensured.

What an intoxication of hustle, for a man who once hawked tickets to his own fight and even helped a kid sell Ali sweatshirts to show how a pro did it. He has turned the biggest issues of his time, race hatred and war, into a multi-million gate. And as the fans, all those Sinatras and Ethel Kennedys, swarm into the Garden, and as the barflies with blood in their eyes jam the closed-circuit theatres, a veteran observer like Jimmy Jacobs finds his hands sweating. "That never happened to me before." Ali can do that; at the first Liston fight, the stone gargoyles who sit in the front row and look as if they are painted on the seats, were up and shouting. But that was nothing compared with tonight.

"How can you get so sore at Ali?" I ask someone. "It's just a gag."

"I hate him," someone says simply.

"OK, but how can you love Frazier? He's a pug, like any other. Name three important differences between him and Joe Palooka."

For answer I have to content myself with the burning gaze of the zealot. Ali has not only remodelled himself but his opponent as well. He has told us what to feel

Ali at Frazier's camp before the first fight.

119

and how strongly to feel it. He has orchestrated us all. Well, I'm damned if I'm going to be pushed around like this myself. I will not be part of his con. I admire Ali's ring technique—*that's* why I'm rooting for him. Temperately and in good taste.

As the fight approaches, my palms are sweating too.

To have all this and a great fight as well is too much to ask of an imperfect world. Yet we got the greatest. Ali's pride demanded it, and Frazier's skill was equal to it. No one has ever fought better than Smokin' Joe that night. Most fights, like most books, contain one or two good ideas at the beginning and a lot of puffing and

blowing in the later stages. But Frazier was still able to fell trees in the 15th round, and Ali was still able to dissuade him from it. In fact, that round alone was worth the price of most fights.

The immediate question was, what was Ali going to use in place of legs. He was still fast, but not superhumanly so, and Frazier bounds in at an agile, tireless trot that even the old Ali would have had to stop and confront at some point. The new Ali was down to hand-speed and intelligence, of which he has enough.

His early plan seemed to be to hit Joe with lightning combinations and then tie him up. The clinch was a comparatively new weapon for him, not to mention the head-in-the-armpit hold, but he took to these old man's devices with a resigned ease. Of course, no one plan can last 15 rounds against the likes of Frazier and before the fight was over, Ali had improvised a whole grammar of styles.

"I'm going to fight ten more years and people still won't know if I can take a punch," Ali said once. "I'm not in there to prove whether I can take a punch." But that night, he reluctantly proved it, again and again. At times he made Frazier a gift of his mid-section to protect his head. But he made some mistakes with his head too, and Frazier came in with some shuddering shots over missed right leads. Each time, Ali found some way to show wobbly derision. He couldn't just take a punch—he could take one better than anyone who'd ever lived. Incredulously we watched as he reluctantly unwrapped perhaps his greatest gift. Courage.

By the middle rounds, Frazier was dom-

inating the fight in that mystical sense which makes scorekeeping an interpretive art. You can dominate from the ropes or you can dominate from the center of the ring; you can do it running or you can do it standing still. You don't even have to land the most punches (by count, Frazier didn't even come close). All you have to do is call the tune and assert your will.

When a man like Frazier does this, it is usually just a question of guessing the round. Yet, after each one, Ali managed to summon a sneer and a mocking flip of the hand. He would not be dominated *psychologically* so long as one brain cell remained lit. He would at least be on top between rounds.

During the mid-game, Ali took to jiggling his fist in Frazier's face and smirking, another Ali first. Later on, it enabled him to say he shouldn't have played games like that, but it looked at the time like a council of desperation, a calculated use of his superior reach to keep Frazier off him for a few healing moments. It did not spare him a terrible beating. Frazier would slap once, twice, at the offending fist and then would leap past it with a murderous hook. It became like a schoolyard game: how many slaps before the real one.

Ali could no longer dance out of range so he took to resting against the ropes and nesting his head in his gloves like peek-a-boo Floyd Patterson, while Frazier pounded him with rib-crushing body blows. Some rest. "Kill the body and the head will die": boxing's most revered maxim also took a beating that night.

By round ten or so, we were learning to live with not one but two miracles. Ali

123

was still on his feet and Frazier was still smoking. Joe had landed his best shot and Ali had done his jelly-leg stagger—being a clown has its uses. He was damn near out but Frazier didn't know it.

After that they would both have been excused for waltzing out the clock in time-honored style. Most fighters would have had no choice. Yet incredibly the best of the fight was still to come. A third miracle occurred: out of God knows what resources, Ali found the strength to come back, and Frazier's face began to wash away under Ali's snapping jabs. In the 15th, Joe came back with a killer left hook, Ali's old enemy, and it appeared over. The dedicated Ali watcher, Eddie Futch, had come up with a new trick. When Ali commences an upper-cut, he leaves his whole right side exposed; so Futch had advised Frazier to move in, let the uppercut graze off his stomach, and unload. And unload he did. It says much for Joe that he could wait 15 rounds for this situation to arise, and still have the kitchen sink in readiness. My back teeth still sing at the memory of that punch. But Ali got up somehow and fought in a coma for a few seconds and then, my God, launched a counterattack of sorts as the fight ended. They have given Congressional Medals of Honor for less. "I hope they appreciated my artistry," said Ali.

The scoring of fights is, as indicated, a mystic pursuit, depending on how one interprets dominance, but the consensus is that Ali's greatest fight was ironically a defeat. Referee Arthur Mercante gave Frazier eight rounds, Ali six, and one for the pot, and the ref usually knows best, especially if he's Mercante.

Both fighters left the ring as slightly different people. Forty-five minutes' work

can do that in this business. Frazier left his greatness behind—that witch's brew of talent and passion, of physical and mental vitality—and became merely sporadically excellent. As a public figure, he deflated instantly, until such time as Ali chose to pump him up again for their next fight. People love or hate Frazier entirely in relation to Ali; otherwise they have no feelings about him whatsoever. The non-fight fans

who yearned for him till the sweat ran that night have probably not given him a thought since.

As for Ali, another change of persona is no news for him. The public hatred which he'd so carefully nursed came to a head that night and burst and may never be the same. To some people, he went back to being an irritation, to others he was suddenly a familiar institution, like other young rogues whose badness has been blessed by time, but very few people hated him anymore. The old-timers would never like him, but they loved boxing and they'd seen the best. Can a ballet fan really hate Nureyev? They may also have felt the mixed respect they'd feel for a fag who beats up a bar or wins the Legion of Honor—a respect tinged with pleasure. Above all, they'd seen him beaten, that great healer of hate, and they'd seen the Mick Jagger smirk smashed off his face.

Ali's lack of conventional masculinity may have bothered his critics' psyches more than his race and his youth. Who can read the heart of a critic? If so, the cat was out of the bag now. Ali was no specimen of the unisex counter-culture but an old-fashioned lion-hearted hero. Ho hum. The publicity freak has met his greatest challenge: Acceptance.

Can he handle it? His career enters another bleak phase. His critics have fallen to debating like medieval theologians over whether the old Ali wouldn't have been beaten even worse by Frazier—the kind of argument they have about old retired athletes. He has been defused. Meanwhile, Frazier has entered upon the cumbersome dance of the champions, in which fighters strain every nerve to avoid meeting each other. It looks as if Ali will not get another

crack at the Belt in what's left of his prime.

Offstage, the Vietnam question has cooled still further, so that Ali's draft evasion looks no worse than Jack Dempsey's after World War I. And Elijah, urged on by his businesslike sons, has announced some kind of détente with Whitey. The problem is not the oppressor, says he, but us. (Ah, what Pogo has wrought.) All this good will tarnishes Ali's image. Whoever heard of Public Enemy No. 2? It will take a public relations miracle to bring his hate-ability back. Or is there something else he can do?

Perhaps there is, but he doesn't stumble on it right away. Grimly Ali rejoins the chain gang of contenders, fighting such fellow-stragglers as Jimmy Ellis and Joe Bugner at regular intervals like a working stiff. Again he must tread water while waiting for a title shot, and in the course of this listless occupation, his skill seems to slip once more, presumably for the last time.

He fights Bob Foster, a light heavyweight and his mind seems to be on something else, until Foster cuts him for the first time and Ali wakes up and dispatches him. Maybe he needs these alarm clocks now. He goes in against a relative unknown called Ken Norton and is defeated. True, he has not bothered to train; true (or not true) he has fought the last ten rounds with a broken jaw. Still, his stock drops further. An aging fighter cannot make these mistakes.

Not because they prove anything conclusively but because they hurt his promotability. What happened against Norton might have happened at any stage of Ali's career, but promoters don't always know things like that. Ali's old nemesis, Eddie

131

Futch, the demon trainer, was in Norton's corner and he had a new trick up his sleeve, like the Joker in *Batman* comics. He figured that Ali was so proud of his fast jab that if you jab back more or less simultaneously, he will be nonplussed.

And so it came to pass. Simple as it seems, this tactic is very unorthodox and Ali could not adjust to it. Norton held up his right glove to protect against Ali's left and shot his own back into the empty space. And Ali thought Norton's jab was actually faster than his. It wasn't, says Futch, but it didn't have to be. Ali's vanity was stung and his poise shaken. At some point his jaw was indeed broken, but most observers agree that it happened too late to affect the result, and that the event was moved back retroactively to the second round by the active mind of Dundee.

So Ali hadn't regressed as much as we vultures supposed. But his fingers had slipped an inch on the greasy slope, and much of his work was sluggish during this period. The only thing to be said for it was that there was a lot of it. He fought every few months, possibly on the theory that if he got out of training he'd never get back, and much of it was like watching inferior reruns, against old friends like Chuvalo and Cooper and Patterson, the old heavyweight stock company.

Worse still, the work of the publicity freak was uninspired. To some extent, it was still harnessed to his boxing—and all the lip in the world couldn't save a dull fight. But more seriously, his routine had no place to go as theater. The boasting had become a national institution. Small kids could do it, along with their W.C. Fields imitations. The poems from the Ali factory were as alike in quality as fortune cookies. The predictions had ceased altogether. Nowadays Ali was as likely to praise an opponent (usually in inverse proportion to his talent) as mock him. And his tiffs with the press were sometimes downright kittenish. "Dick Young, you are the *trickiest* writer," he might say after a rough column, until even his enemies were charmed.

It was still a good show, but it needed something. It depended heavily on boyishness, and boyishness can turn sour on you, as we saw with Willie Mays. It was also too unambiguously likeable, which meant one could only take a few minutes of it. There was no dramatic tension anymore.

Ali finally got his second shot at Frazier, though only after Frazier had lost the championship to Foreman, and this gave him a chance to relive the unpleasantness of the first fight and perhaps rekindle public hatred. Frazier magically became a white man again—although his life has been the Negro reality, and Ali's only the Negro dream—and Ali called him dumb and

Don King consoles Ali after loss to Norton, 1973.

136

(preceding page) *The second Frazier fight.*

Ali and Belinda in Zaire.

was like watching Astaire and Rogers doubled with arthritis. We had seen the last of Ali the great fighter for sure, so we forgave the mess with Frazier.

The writers by now were as worn out with myth-making as Ali himself, and were just clinging and hanging on. He needed new writers as much as new opponents, and he badly needed to get out of the sports pages—a tight cage for a super-celebrity. For instance, there was no way he could get the sports boys that interested in his spiritual growth, for all the clues he was giving them.

The answer, and it was an inspired one, was Africa. The Dark Continent, where many a westerner, from Stanley to Schweitzer to Hemingway has rediscovered himself. Also, the Third World with a billion (who's counting?) new fans for the taking. Adoration like unto Boulder Dam. He already has his Muslim connections (although I suspect the sheiks were more impressed to meet a heavyweight champ than just another Black Muslim) and it only remained to cash them. While passing through Kuwait, he casually agreed with President Mobutu of Zaire to hold a fight at his place. So a championship date was set with George Foreman for five big ones in the new Republic of Zaire.

He couldn't have picked a better symbol. Zaire, or the old Belgian Congo, was the very heart of emerging Africa. In fact, it was such a good symbol that some American blacks couldn't stand it. I'm told that by African standards it is in pretty good shape, considering that the Belgians did everything but rip out the telephones before leaving. But emerging nations are generally best admired at a distance. Ali's entourage had not signed on to swat flies in the jungle,

fake-wrestled him on television, and maybe it stirred some sluggish bile in the Ali-haters. But it was more messy than spectacular. Frazier wrote an aggrieved article in *Ebony* about how he'd helped Ali in the bad years, and if his annoyance was on the level, it only made one uncomfortable. Ali had hurt an old friend's feelings by straining too hard for effect. It was like middle-aged men roughhousing. Not funny, not tragic, just infinitely forgettable.

Also, this hairy build-up required a great fight to justify it, and the old boys could no longer provide one. The second Ali-Frazier fight was not a bad fight, once you got used to the clinching and head-holding. But if you'd seen the original, it

140

and they avoided the local life as much as possible. "A backward Haiti" one of them called it. And even Ali was heard to observe that he would rather be in Miami.

So as a goodwill tour it was pretty much of a bust for most parties. The writers clung to their hotel in Kinshasa, and the fight people to their camps. Remember—Ali's followers had been living pretty high on the hog, and were still busy outracing whatever poverty they'd known; they might talk a good game about the ghetto, but tagging along with the champ is an excellent way of keeping out of it. Thus, returning to a pre-Sears Roebuck culture was an unacceptable strain, and the kind of social communion that would have made the trip a real triumph rather than a paper one never happened.

To make things worse, the fight got postponed by a freak cut over Foreman's eye, which meant that a super rock concert that had been planned to coincide with the fight went off early to a near empty stadium, at least by rock concert standards, where audiences are counted in quarter millions. The most expensive talent in America blew their hearts out for two straight nights to a handful of puzzled Africans before opening the gates for free on the third and last, with Zaire gloomily picking up the tab.

Altogether, a trip to forget. Yet Ali somehow managed to make it a personal triumph—all the shinier for being set in a disaster. Although the total package cost Zaire a bundle in money and bad will, Ali himself emerged as a black world leader as never before. What he personally thought of Zaire is curiously beside the point. The consensus is that he had to force himself to like it at all. He is a fastidious man, as well kept as a great estate tended by gardeners, and he is a child of technology, a twentieth century American to the bone, shuttling between phone and tube.

Yet he managed to drum up a species of love affair with Zaire, at least on their side: one reason being that they loved him already, but the other being that he really sees himself as a black Kissinger, who works on his diplomacy as carefully as on everything else. He'd been to Africa twice before, in 1964 and 1966 (when he'd been a somewhat more Spartan character himself) and had absorbed what you do with the people and what you do with the leader. Added to the politeness his mama taught him, this gives you intermittently the prettiest American, in a world of quiet, ugly ones, and quite possibly the best potential representative we have, since *all* the outside world, even the white one, tends to be mesmerized by black Americans.

But he had more on his mind right now than just generating more love. He also had a fight to think about—against a man

who had lifted Joe Frazier clear off his feet and had left him for dead in two, and had literally paralyzed Ken Norton with fear before dispatching him in another two. This dreamy assassin was training just up the street, a palpable presence. It was hard to concentrate on being an ambassador-at-large, a black Kissinger, with George Foreman in town.

Yet Ali wondrously managed to combine his two objectives into one bizarre triumph. He won the hearts and minds of the Zaireans and turned them into a weapon against lonesome George; and then he turned his success in the ring into a quasi-religious celebration of himself.

How does he do it? If I knew I'd be King of Dublin. For this one, it all has to be done in his spare time, of which training for Foreman doesn't leave you much. There is airy talk of triumphal tours through the countryside but few of them seem to come off. Outside of three dutiful visits to the ill-starred rock festival, his entertaining time is mostly confined to the happy few

who can jam into his gym every day.

Yet he makes a little go a long way. When he does appear publicly at a mass rally with Foreman and Mr. Mobutu, he does it all, from the great man shuffle and the kind nobleman gaze (love, with dignity) to the body language of the platform. His time as a preacher and lecturer serves him well: his style of incantation makes the body sway and the voice want to shout back. The fact that the Zaireans don't understand a word of it doesn't seem to hurt a bit. They dig the sound all the more for being undeflected by meaning.

The occasion is a dedication of the renovated stadium of Kinshasa, which Mobutu is donating "to the people," whatever that means; but the event of the day is Ali's stately arrival. But what must the crowd have been thinking as they roared? All that excitement—but for what? A boxing match? The only fresh subjects in sight were Ali and Foreman, and Foreman isn't the kind of thing you chant about unless you've got a lot of time on your hands. They gave him the kind of ovation you'd give any heavyweight who was passing through; but Ali got the works, the primal scream, the great getting up morning hello. But what were they screaming for? Not a god, or a king precisely. Not a black man—they'd seen those before. Not even a celebrity anymore. He was just an Ali. One of a kind. Pure transcendence.

We're used to Ali by now, but in a spanking new country, he may have appeared as a symbol of deliverance and black hope; or he may have just seemed like a great American entertainer. It doesn't matter. The message beamed to the world and to Ali was that he was a leader among his people. A crowd is a crowd, never mind

Mrs. Cassius Clay Sr.

what it's thinking. Ali's legend marched on, and Zaire was on the map—a fair exchange. Who was the last fighter to teach us the name of a new country?

At the same time, the fun and games of Dundee and Bundini were keeping the pot boiling in their own ways. The hexes and hoaxes of boxing fit in admirably with the mumbo jumbo legends of Africa, and in no time rumors were flying of witch doctors and double-dish curses. At first, I figured this was just Dundee dressed up in a sheet, and that the visitors were making it all up to sell the fight. But checking it out with an African expert, I find that there is enough real sorcery in Zaire to make it more than just a white man's gag. Zaire abounds in witch doctors, although some of them are just herbalists who can't do a thing to your enemies, and others are more like clergymen, who plug you into the divine will with no money-back miracles. The process is pentecostal, a passing on of the Spirit; stuff you can get in Bayonne, N.J.

However, there's no point sanitizing it too much for the western mind. The city-dwellers of Kinshasa may wink at it like city-Christians, but in the country there's still plenty of down-home voodoo, complete with devil possession. And Mr. Mobutu himself keeps a lucky dwarf. Having outlawed Christianity (an important point for Ali), he may want to encourage folk religions, however outlandish.

Which suited Dundee and Bundini and the promoters just fine. Africa has always been fair game for white man's razzle-dazzle, and the promotion of this fight belongs to a long line of Tarzan adventures and Clark Gable jungle-grunts. The natives helped out by placing little bags of herbs

under the ring, as they do behind the goal posts in soccer matches, and exhorting their private witch doctors to root Ali home anyway they knew how.

Very funny. But it seems ironic that this event, which was supposed to call attention to an earnest young Third World country, should wind up advertising its hairiest superstitions. Granted that there's only so much you can say about new highways and power plants—and it was said over and over—one had a feeling that the westerners were up to their old tricks, using the blacks for cheap entertainment.

For the promoters, pushing their latest tom-tom spectacular, this was understandable. But how did Ali the Muslim get mixed up in it? Several times he made Little Black Sambo fun of his hosts, for American consumption. For instance, I doubt the Zaireans were amused to hear that they

143

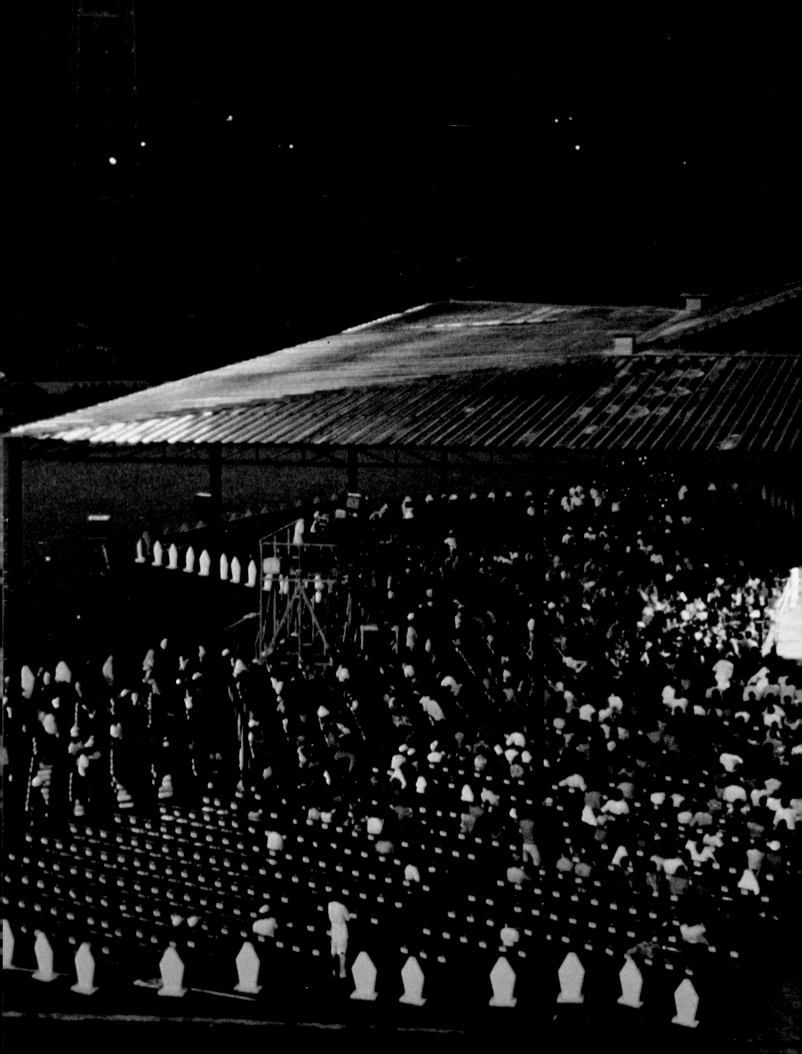

were going to boil George Foreman in a pot (in fact to judge from photographs, I doubt they're amused by much). He also said, for pressmen to hear, that the native pilots must carry little white men in boxes to fly the planes. As for his famous slogan, "We're going to rumble in the jungle," Kissinger would never have said that, against the slick skyline of Kinshasa. All of Ali's solemn posing with Mobutu and the people can be blown by a few blasts from the Punk.

So there is still a real alienation between his promotional self and his burning desire to be serious, which Zaire highlights as never before. But this is his problem not theirs. They are enjoying a break in a hard lifetime, and they thrill to such sideshows as Bundini's cry of *"Ali boma ye,"* which they shout back cheerfully. They've already got a leader and then some, but where do you find such entertainers? Our celebrity can wrestle with his soul on his own time, as far as they're concerned.

But for Ali, this is an agitating period. Besides the ever-growing burdens of sanctity, which could cause shooting pains every time he sees a woman, there is a need to win, beyond anything since Frazier. He is 32 now and making his last big roll. Besides, he believes that the red-necks always wanted him to "go home to Africa and get his ass whupt," and he absolutely cannot give them satisfaction. So he trains down to a point where a touch on the shoulder can make him a killer. He has some kind of a spat (rumors fly like pigeons) with his quiet wife Belinda and she leaves Africa sporting a George Foreman button (only to return shortly). He slaps Bundini in the dressing room, hard enough to startle George Plimpton, who has seen everything. And on his way to the ring, observers say

he even appears to smack his brother Rachaman. Maybe for luck.

These untypical outbursts are a measure of the psychic strain he has laid on himself. Later, preparing for the likes of Wepner, he is the safest man in the world to be around. Ali normally prides himself on being the gentlest of fighters—how else can a Muslim justify his calling—but viciousness is a tool of the trade, and he is going to need every tool in the bag against Foreman. This, remember, is a man who can maim and disfigure him, or snap his cortex until his cerebrum rattles, starting him on the road to brain damage; conversely, a victory over George will crown his career with impossible glory. So the one weapon he has never needed—killer instinct—is taken from its case and honed, just in case.

For once in his life, Ali becomes almost decipherable. The specter of defeat clearly hounds him. Everyday he asks reporters what the odds are. Two-and-a-half to one against, they tell him. He pretends not to care, then asks again the next day. He spends more and more time with individual writers, as if trying for one last huge gulp of publicity before he goes under.

He hectors the reporters to bet on him, and calls them fools for picking Foreman, as if he can beat the odds down with his tongue. He acts out scenarios which cannot fail, and hints at further scenarios too devastating to mention. His mind darts about like a trapped animal; then subsides, according to its own rhythms. He says that he has one edge over his rival which cannot fail. "Foreman has never tasted defeat." Your reporter has heard all he needs to hear: he puts his money on George.

If there is any fear left from Ali's childhood, he must have felt it throbbing in those last days. He has already tortured himself to maximum sharpness when Foreman's cut caused the postponement, so he has to torture himself all over again. A non-participant is awed by how he converts fear to rage as part of his training. But perhaps every fighter can do this. What every fighter *cannot* do is keep his public image tuned like a Stradivarius at the same time.

But Ali does it somehow, by a virtuoso use of temperament, as strange as anything in sports history. The crowd at the gym still gets a full matinee every day from rope skipping to rant, which is tailored to African needs by now. Ali also seems to have the inside track with Mobutu, although the leader has declared official neutrality. Ali hits it off with strong men, with his style of almost exaggerated respectfulness, and of all the strong men in his life, Mobutu has to be tops. I asked my African adviser if Mr. M has any domestic political opposition and he said "none," and we know how that's usually done. Elijah himself never got so far. Mobutu is also far and away the biggest landowner in Zaire, a real all round president.

Nevertheless, it is uphill work for Ali to make himself the biggest national cause since independence. Publicly Mobutu is tickled to have two black men fighting in a black country and has signs up everywhere proclaiming it. May the best black man win. As for George Foreman, he blends very nicely with the jungle—he doesn't *look* like a white boy. Yet for the sake of Ali's adrenaline, he must become one, one more time; Ali's cause must be *everyone's* cause, and his victory must be a matter of national urgency. He must see to it that every Zairean has a personal stake

in him, to be converted into a Bund rally roar at George.

For years, he's been able to work this trick with political activists ("He's got to win," says Bernadette Devlin, "he's *got* to win.") even when he's fighting a Liston or a Frazier, the kind of Negro who really has had a raw deal from life. But how on earth is he going to do it here? How does a fair-skinned, middle-class (at least on alternate days), very American-looking Negro, go about claiming to be the only black man in the ring—and claim it in a foreign language?

"These are my people, I ain't leaving," he says, when Foreman has threatened to call the fight off—which is a neat way out of saying he needs the fight more than Champion George. But I believe this mostly goes down with his black American audience. To win the Zaireans, he has to connect with their essence, and become what they would like to be themselves, as opposed to an unattainable foreigner, like Foreman or most black Americans.

At this point, meditating on the hundreds of pictures I've seen, I fantasize a religious ceremony, featuring Ali in African robes, and a voodoo priest who turns out to be Bundini. Suddenly the crowd begins to cheer wildly as an actual African king enters Ali's soul—where it meets the Muslim preacher and laughing boy to produce the strange effect I feel in Cleveland. Too much. But Ali is such a quick study that he may have picked up just a piece of Mobutu to go with his Cosell. All one knows for sure is that these moments of controlled fear and confusion, against Liston, Frazier and Foreman, have each signalled a major change of character and direction. That is a real furnace he passes

through each time, and it shapes and hardens.

Whether this mutation actually occurred in time to rally the Zaireans—or whether, like the more developed peoples, they are simply besotted by famous names—Ali had the whole nation in his corner by fight time. Africans are traditionally a warm, expressive people and Ali certainly *appears* to be that, if you aren't familiar with American synthetics. And they like a man who likes to talk. Even in his pet Arabic, he only knows words like "hello, sheik and goodbye." But they like the way his lips keep moving. To some extent he wins these matches by default, against fur-tongued opposition. I should like before he quits to see him up against another Ali.

Anyway, whether the Zaireans loved him for his blackness or for himself, he had, for his own frame of mind, to consider the fight a black crusade, even though there was no one in sight but more blacks. Travel can be spiritually disorienting (Englishmen who go to California never recover) and can induce quasi-mystical states you don't

get at home. So if you add the strangeness of Africa to a condition of preternatural terror and determination, and a fervent belief in Allah, you have something that would blow the average mind and at least make a ripple in Ali's.

But meanwhile, he was training very intelligently for the fight, working his peak hours round the clock gradually so that he could box at four in the morning without seeming as if he just got out of bed. His gym work is generally misleading. Like most great fighters, he doesn't mind exposing his weaknesses in order to work on them better. Unless you know exactly what he's up to, he can look as if he's lost his grip completely. But it might have been noted for our instruction that Ali was taking an awful lot of shots to the belly for a man who planned to dance all night.

Most of the talk was about his dancing and how long he could keep it up. Back in 1970, a journeyman named Gregorio Peralta had made a monkey out of Foreman with good lateral movement, and maybe Ali could do the same. But Foreman had learned a thing or two since (I wouldn't put the number higher than that), and he had two of the shrewdest old champs in his corner, Archie Moore thirsting for Ali's blood, and Sandy Saddler to tell him which direction Ali was last seen in.

I placed my bet with a local body repairman, who was also wagering the whole black community around here that Ali would win. He tapped his forehead. "He's a head fighter," he explained. Well, that was one thing going for him. There was probably no easy way to beat him. One felt he could turn into a puff of smoke if pressed. The other was that Foreman liked to get his fights over quickly and might begin to pout after the third round.

It wasn't nearly enough on Ali's side of the scale. Besides, the body man was offering 2 to 1. It is a testament to how much one had identified with Ali that I made the bet with misgivings and a heavy heart (as such things go)—and was delighted when I lost it. "That's all right," said the body man next day. "I never saw so many people happy to lose money."

Because Ali turned his miracle that night—the one he'd gambled his whole divinity on. After a bizarre dressing room scene which has already been described like the Last Supper by Mailer and Plimpton, and which includes the famous slapping of disciple Bundini (there was a falling-out over which robe the champ should wear), Ali strode out and crowned himself.

It was decidedly not another fight of the century (the rule is no more than one of those to a decade). In fact, placed back to back with the first Frazier film, it looks like a Looney Tunes cartoon: Ali fought like a normal man from time to time, and even like an inspired one, with the surprise right leads he perfected as far back as the Golden Gloves, but most of the time he just lay back on the ropes, which were slack as Christmas bunting, and did nothing at all. Later he says he planned this strategy all along, but if so, it is news to his trainer Dundee, who is still shaking his head about it hours after the fight. The fact is, if it hadn't been an Occasion, it would have been a bore; and much more of this would kill boxing for sure.

But Ali had made it an Occasion, and the big news, mysteriously important, was that he won at all, never mind how. His cause had totally eclipsed boxing—whatever the devil his cause was. Small children felt it; Kurds and Welshmen and the higher primates felt it. *Ali boma ye.* Something good has happened to our people.

To return to earth for a moment, and the drab technicalities: Ali had worked out a serviceable scenario, which depended on the fathomless unimaginativeness of George. He was right to feel nervous and call on Allah, because Saddler and Moore were hard at work trying to pump imagination into their boy.

In the early days, Moore had worked with Ali briefly, before balking at his sassiness and contempt for other men's ideas, and he knew as much about Ali as a wise old fighter can know. And Saddler had beaten the great Willie Pep, of whom it was said that his glove could appear in one corner while his feet were in another—fast even by Ali's standards. Never has so much savvy been assembled in one corner. But they couldn't pass it on to George. Round after round, he went out and made the same mistakes, attacking Fortress Ali frontally instead of from the sides and pawing for his head like a clumsy bear, trying to get Ali to hold still for a moment. Angelo Dundee had observed that Foreman cannot move to his right without getting his legs tangled, so that was something else for the big grizzly to worry about. He is also a sucker for hand and head feints, and indeed movement of any kind.

All in all an embarrassing time for George. And embarrassment is as exhausting as any other emotion. George began to tire suspiciously early, and people watching on closed-circuit TV thought he was dogging it intentionally. But nobody in the arena thought that. They had heard his punches go off like shotgun blasts in the early rounds, and were amazed that Ali's

tripes weren't jumbled beyond repair. A lot of these punches had been blocked by Ali's arms, but even arms are made of flesh and bone, and most people couldn't lift theirs after two rounds of Foreman.

There's a saying in boxing that if any fighter had to go 15 rounds with the heavy punching bag, the heavy bag would win. George went eight. A boxer even slightly out of shape quickly unravels and becomes one of us. And George, while more than fit enough for his usual two-round work-outs, had been observed chasing a girl round a swimming pool that afternoon, training a la Harpo. So he finally succumbed to heat and embarrassment and a few *pro forma* Ali punches. As it must to all of us, bedtime came to George Fore-man—at four o'clock in the morning, Zaire time. There was a mix-up over the count, which only might have given a small hype to the next fight: Ali's fights are like movie serials, always leaving a question to be solved next time. Get your tickets now.

The count issue did not get off the ground, but what about those loose ropes? By arching his back against them, Ali was able to remove his head altogether from the plane of George's punches. Could he have done this with normal ropes? And if not, who loosened the ropes? Not that little imp Dundee again?

The ropes certainly were funny look-ing. In fact when I saw the films, the people I was with burst out laughing. Dundee says that he actually tried to tighten them, but the hemp was sodden and limp (one nice thing about Angelo is that he doesn't mind if you don't believe him; but the argument here is not between Dundee and the rainy season, but whether the ropes affected the outcome). For the defense, Dave Anderson

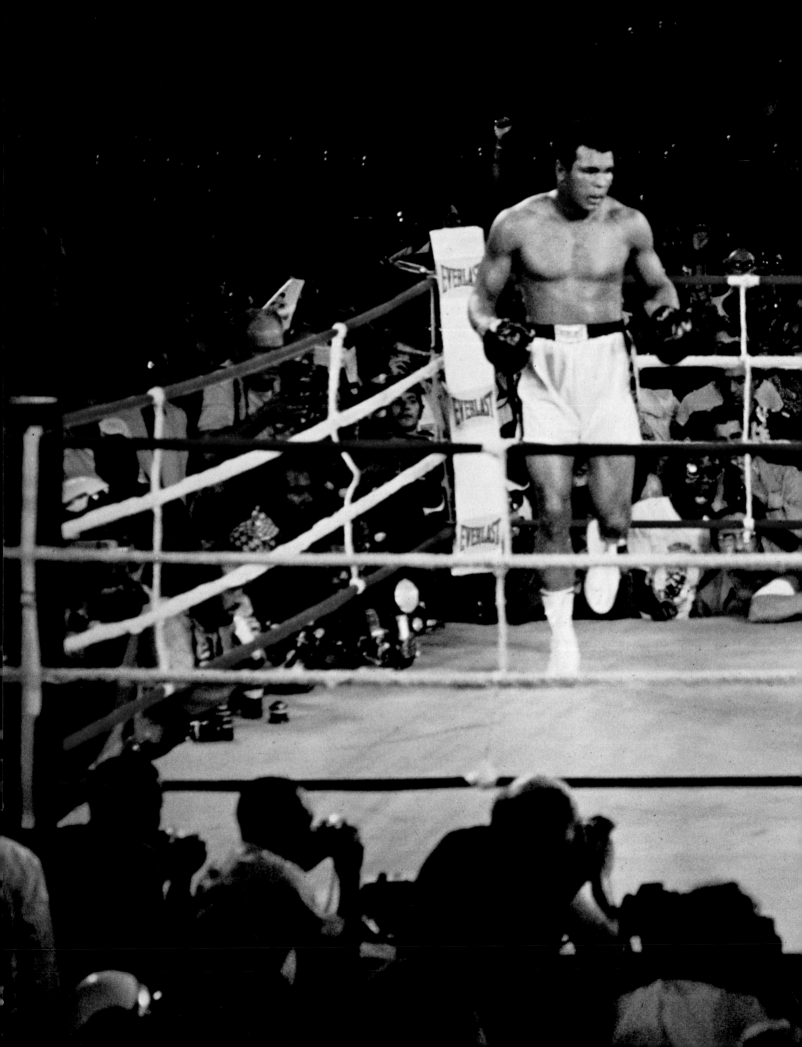

of the *Times* suggests that ropes that loose could actually be a hazard to the man leaning against them, increasing his chances of flying through or over them. But the Ali myth suddenly seemed beyond such arguments. His believers knew he would think of *something*, and he did.

Ali's critics were by now down to a straggle of refugees, riddled with desertion. All they had left was the theory that all his major fights were fixed. One of our finest sportswriters (I'd say our very finest, but that would identify him) put it to me that Ali might now be so important to boxing that boxing couldn't afford to have him lose, an argument that casts a quick shadow over the fun. But Mr. Smith (we'll call him that to protect his anonymity) admitted he

had seen the fight on TV with Jack Dempsey, who despises Ali in the name of all that's holy. And he added that he knows of only two people in the world who agree with him, neither of whom was in Africa that night, and one of whom is always wrong.

So Ali's superiority was now about as acknowledged as it is ever going to be. Foreman later said he'd been drugged and it was too hot and what all, but no one was listening. "It wasn't the African weather, it was the Ali leather," says the bard. And the bard knows.

If he had screamed after Liston, he must have wanted to howl after this one. And one pictures him standing in the ring, chanting to his people, wanting the moment to last forever. King of the jungle now, for sure. But unfortunately he collapsed from exhaustion himself, only a few moments behind Foreman. Maybe his willpower would have carried him another round or so, but an African night full of body punches and psychic phenomena had drained him and he was closer to defeat than anyone knew. He couldn't even manage the 80 or so stanzas of verse that he recited from ringside the night of the second Frazier fight.

So he left the joint testily, having missed his celebration, and with nothing to look forward to but the usual Muslim orange juice binge. Instead of rejoicing the old way, he snapped at reporters for not believing in him. Maybe his nerves are more complicated than they used to be, and joy doesn't come on demand. But he was punctual and sharp as a diamond at the next morning's press conference. And the state of his soul right then must have been something to see. He had accomplished something even *he* didn't believe in. If one tries to reduce this to coherent thoughts, it is a writer's fiction. A weather map would be closer to it, full of turbulence and high pressure and storm warnings. My God, he'd done it: he had his championship again, the Holy Grail he'd been seeking since youth, and which had been ripped off him by the white man. His last and worstest dragon had staggered mumbling from the ring, and there was nothing more to be done.

How do you come down from a high like that? Can you just go back to being a nice guy with a big mouth? He has seen a fairer vision than that, a veritable transfiguration. But how to capture it again?

The Evelyn Waugh brigade pulls out, leaving Zaire in the dustbin of history, and Ali has to face the morning after. He is a different kind of celebrity now—one can tell by the way people talk about him. Serious people ask me what his plans are. Word goes round that he's really super-intelligent. His intellectual supporters pray that it is so.

All these gases swirl around the head of our hero, a man not normally given to linear thought. Ali picks up vibes beautifully, but doesn't always know what to do with them. And his new fame is so strange and amorphous that the finest mind might have trouble with it.

By all accounts, his intuition can go places where reason is barred. But so far, this superb instrument has been dedicated solely to what's best for him. Now, as the world's leading celebrity-at-large, he must have other responsibilities. But what are they? He senses that the Third World is crucial to his image, so he quickly and creditably offers to help it along. He senses,

less clearly, that racism must remain part of the act, because it was central to his great moments, of championship lost and regained, and because it is the only serious subject he knows anything about. His mama didn't raise him to sing his own praises all day, so he makes the Black Race his surrogate. And his Muslim identity continues to add that touch of mystery and menace.

What he seems less sure about since Zaire is his personal deportment. Some sort of seriousness is in order, and we get the young statesman at the UN. But what portions do we assign now to basic decency and honest rage? How much is moody genius and how much is Mr. Nice? Remember—these are not conscious decisions, only the actor's instinctive groping as he learns a new part. What do the folks expect? What's the *right* thing to do (that's certainly part of it)? How do I stay on top?

It is possible that his great ring career ended that night, leaving him to crumbs like Wepner and finally defeat at the hands of an equal, in a dull split decision. He'll have to talk to his body about that. It still looks capable of anything, but bodies have minds of their own.

History doesn't care too much one way or the other. The drama of exile and return is now complete. From draft board to Zaire, he has acted out, on a pop-art scale, the story we all long to believe of death and rebirth and vindication. Ali has entered folklore and has no place to go but down.

Unless, that is, he can get another myth started. At the moment he is taking his first stuttering steps, right here in Cleveland, that town of fickle lustre, while the old myth tugs at his sleeve like the ghost of Christmas past and the new one lies before him, a blank black void.

Looking Glass Country

The Dark Side

The Bleeder is duly bled. Chuck Wepner is dragged to his corner like a dead bull, after 15 rounds of torture—mental and facial.

Anyone who's forgotten that this is a bloody business Ali's engaged in is set straight by a quick look at Wepner's punctured veins and the red stains on his trunks. A few feet away, Dave Anderson's typewriter is still caked with George Chuvalo's blood, courtesy of your favorite pacifist. Ali has caused as much bloodshed as any war veteran. The pre-fight gags and glitter are prelude to a pig sticking.

In the circumstances, Ali's cornermen, Dundee, Pacheco, Bundini and Youngblood, look like a Red Cross team in their little white coats—which makes it all the more peculiar when Bundini starts acting like the wild man from Borneo in the late rounds. He just doesn't seem dressed right.

The moment these four enter the ring, it is like the MGM lion roaring; an Ali production would not look right without them. For fifteen rounds, or whatever it takes, they will move around Ali like marionettes, wetting him, drying him and giving him fruitless advice.

Ali has time to fight like a celebrity tonight, putting on a one-man show. And if you haven't seen him before, it is pretty impressive at first. From the front row he looks twice as fast as he looks on screen, proving among other things that legs can come back. He seems to circle overhead like a maddened carousel, uttering those strange cries, somewhere between a "tcha" and a "pfoo" that fighters use to tighten their stomach muscles (every fighter does this, but Ali's grunts easily drown the other guy's) while snapping out jabs like a wet towel.

Nevertheless, it is one of Ali's lesser works. Like Picasso painting a potato dumpling, he tries everything he knows but the subject defeats him. Even he has not found a way to eliminate the other fighter altogether from the picture. Worse luck for Narcissus, boxing is not a sport you can play by yourself, however elegantly. What he needs is a Foreman—but right now he doesn't want a Foreman. The title he has clawed his way back to can be lost in minutes. Better to bore the public than that.

163

So for nine rounds he waltzes alone in Ali's dance studios, or rests against the ropes offering Wepner his lower ribs. For theatrics, he mugs like a wrestler whenever Wepner lands a rabbit punch. But this was in the script, he'd decided to do it in advance and his tantrums wouldn't fool a French film critic. In the ninth the aimless Wepner appears to step on Ali's foot and shoot one to the armpit, sending Ali down, after which the champ's anger seems a little more sincere. But if so, Wepner's blood-soaked hulk should appease it nicely. After the glories of Zaire, what is a Wepner here or there?

Time one would suppose for magnanimity. But Ali carries his wrestler's manners into the press conference, lashing out at the referee Tony Perez, a Puerto Rican, and claiming he will never use him again (when fighters get this important, the refs are their employees; Perez unfortunately performed like one tonight, and couldn't control either of his masters). I don't know how much Perez gets paid to be houseboy, but I doubt it's in the area of Ali's 1½ mil; so a coast-to-coast drubbing by the champ seems petty. Doesn't Ali know that he's the King now?

Fighting Wepner at all is undignified enough, but to make a purple scene about it is downright ridiculous. Yet Ali has determined on a scenario of woe, and he sticks to it grimly, even though there seems little chance of his getting disbarred and starting on that second and third comeback tonight. He does succeed in goading Perez into suing him eventually, so his death wish doesn't go away empty-handed.

Of all the turns his character could have taken after Zaire, this is the most surprising. The burden of universal love

suddenly seems too much for him and he wants to pick a fight with someone even after 15 rounds with Wepner. He says that the ref is half white and half black, and is trying to be all white—a slap in the face to Puerto Ricans, who have up to now been his staunchest supporters.

It must have made his true believers slightly queasy to see Ali the friend of Man sticking it to another minority like this. But race is very much on his mind right now, and whatever he has to say about Perez or Wepner or God himself has to be run through the race grinder. It's not enough for Wepner to be a motherbleeper, he has to be a white motherbleeper. And poor Perez has to be a black and white one.

Since all hands agree that Ali is not a natural racist, but has to work at it, this looks like a policy decision. For the uncrowned King of Africa, every fight is a political act. But he has no politics except race. So until he learns another subject, race it is.

He wraps up his surly, grating press conference at last and retires to his dressing room—where, safe in his nest, he takes off his rage like an overcoat and lies prone on the rubbing table. In a soft voice, almost to himself, he tells us he has two bumps on the back of his head, to confirm that he is *so* angry. Fifteen rounds is nightmarish, he says. He recounts his miracles once again. He doesn't sound mad at anybody. The room fills up with brothers and the reporters wander off.

Ali lies beached and becalmed. Body and spirit are drained at last. His words seem to be coming from the base of his spine. Then even that ceases, the moment has come. Ali is too tired to talk. Ferdie Pacheco puts an arm around me. "You

164

wanted to see Ali? You can see him now."

The feeling in the press box is that Ali has made a boo boo about Perez and should try to do better next time. Reporters take a different view of Ali from the rest of the world: like parents, they will never really believe he's a grown-up. Such is their indulgence of Ali's rhetoric by now that he could declare genocide and they'd just shake their heads sadly. Wepner reports that Ali did indeed call him a white unprintable, and we make note of it. The naughty-naughty file bulges like a wastebasket with such items. Once you have a reputation as a bad boy, you can do no wrong.

Yet something in Ali seems to want to challenge this tonight, to raise the ante on hatred. Maybe he misses the days when he was universally despised. Or maybe he simply wants people to take his Muslim ministry seriously—something everyone has steadfastly refused to do so far. My mind goes back to his anti-Christian harangue in Cleveland. This was the clearest indication he has given so far of how he sees his once and future vocation. People keep asking what he's planning to do with himself later, yet when he spells it out like this, their attention wanders. "Muslim preacher" is not the answer they want to hear.

The scene shows the two Alis working together uneasily for the first time, as the new post-Zaire version tries to squeeze his preaching into the cracks in the old Ali's act, while the public stoutly resists this. It all began quite innocently as a poetry exchange with some local schoolchildren. A roomful of kids all ages sits on the floor, as for a picnic or camp meeting. Enter Ali. "Let's see what kind of competition we got here."

He starts out well with the kids, making with the mock menace and the deadpan kidding. "You ain't no poet," he tells one small fry, "you just a itty bitty Joe Frazier." To a skinny fellow, who reads an excellent poem on being black, he says, "Boy, you ain't as dumb as you look."

Suddenly the menace goes too far, as it does in real life, and the children get as confused as we do. His daughter Maryum interrupts, and he says, "The only thing you got on me is you're prettier," which is fine; but then he browbeats her into saying "yes sir" until she bursts into tears. This provides the preacher with an occasion to lecture on the virtues of Muslim women. His daughter will grow up to be real respectable. "I don't want no street-running ladies." But it all begins with learning to say "yes sir."

What are we to feel? This is precisely Ali's art—we don't know what to feel. Our laughter is nervous, our seriousness unsure. "I have been asked to teach philosophy and poetry at Oxford University which is in London [sic], England," he announces next. (He was indeed nominated for the Chair of Poetry at Oxford, which is one of those half-joking, half-serious English things.) The poem he reads on the strength of this is the one that begins "Take two cups of love." The world's greatest university, as he calls it, will never be the same.

"Is my stuff too heavy for you?" he asks the audience. Hardly, it seems. But they didn't come here for uplift. However hard he tries to push the super-serious Ali, everyone wants the old one, the comic strip character. So resignedly, he gives them a burst. "I so pretty they ought to make me a natural resource. You so ugly you ought to be donated to the Government Commission of Wild Life," he tells one luckless waif. Another chap asks why he doesn't knock

out everyone he fights, so Ali points out that even a good-looking dude like the questioner must sometimes strike out with the foxes. "Some of the sisters don't want you. You got your little pimp hat on." What's this? Pimp hat? Is this any way to talk in front of future Muslim ladies? "I'm strong as a bull, there's no girl I can't pull," muses Ali, a million miles from the high-minded scoutmaster of a few minutes back.

He talks about the girls these days like a man picking at a scab. But it is not upmost on his mind today. He's got something else to say, but the preacher can't find an opening. So he just seems vaguely quarrelsome, giving me an idea how opponents feel when the teasing turns mean. Yet officially this is still a pleasant occasion, and he goes through the motions of being pleasant. Children turn him on the way microphones do and he gives a stylized, good-with-children performance that is indeed like Danny Kaye's. One little girl is immune. "I don't like you," she says flatly. He wades into the audience, grabs her and kisses her. That should do it. But when he puts her down, she carefully wipes his kiss off her mouth. This is not calculated to help his mood.

People who think Ali has a fresh speech for every occasion might be surprised by the next part, which is word for word the same as his last press conference, and would be as appropriate in an old people's home as here. He tells the kids how tired he is and all he's accomplished. He reels off fighters they've never heard of, like an old man at a bar. Your respondent trips over his boredom threshold and falls part way asleep. Dimly I hear him say that "their property value goes down when I beat them," and I think, there he goes

166

again; somebody's got to get this man a building permit or he'll go crazy.

Perhaps he's boring himself now and wants to attract his own attention. Because suddenly he is talking in his preacher's voice again about freeing the blacks, and one of the few grown-ups in the audience says, "From what?" It is like a whip-crack and Ali seems slightly flustered. "From the mental chains of slavery," he says. "Oh. *Mental* chains." The woman laughs. She can obviously handle those, the way I can handle spiritual poverty.

That does it. Ali is off and running on his lists of names. If a man is called Rodriguez or Gonzalez we know what he is, right? *(I* don't know what Rodriguez is, Cuban, Argentine, white or black, but let it pass.) If he's called Brezhnev or Khrushchev, we know what he is. But if he's called Smith or Jones or Washington, he could be anybody.

Ali has come here to teach, but the kids seem unmoved by this particular fixation; I've a hunch that they're not about to go out and change their names to Abdul. Again the thing that interests Ali most interests everyone else least. Whether sensing this, or whether it's just that one little word leads to another in his sermons, Ali suddenly switches to a subject that's surefire box office—Jesus Himself, the Big Fellow, the ultimate celebrity that even the Beatles had to pit themselves against before the balloon broke.

Ali wastes no time cutting Him down to size. "When you die you rot, you don't fly no place," he says of Christ's ascension. "How they get him up there?"

While we're into aerodynamics, I'd like to ask about that Muslim spaceship, but he is hurrying along to dispatch both heaven and hell. If hell were down here, it would certainly melt the earth's surface. As for heaven, "There ain't no bees in heaven, makin' honey. Spirits can't eat."

As usual, one is struck by Ali's literalness and his sense of materials. My mind drifts back to a pleasant period of my life when my parents used to speak on street corners for the Catholic church and prayed, on dull or rainy days, for hecklers like Ali to come along, with their literalist attacks on heaven and hell. ("Why is the angels white? The black ones is in the kitchen preparing the Last Supper.") In no time a crowd would roll up to join the fun and the meeting was made.

I remember these hecklers as wiry little men with glasses, hardly Ali's type. Also they *always* had umbrellas, if memory serves me. Yet the patter is achingly familiar. The Virgin Birth? You wouldn't believe your daughter if she came in with a tale like that. You say she got pregnant from leaving the window open? "I know what kind of spook gave *you* the baby." Ali pulls out his shirt to parody pregnancy. "That was one of the brothers who gave you it." He has the little kids laughing now over the Virgin Birth, but some of them are frowning: they've been taught to believe this stuff, and here's the champ saying it ain't so.

Ali then sings a crazy Jesus hymn, which I later find strangely indistinguishable from his imitation of James Brown. All his imitations come out like punch-drunk fighters. On the platform behind him, the man called Blood nods and says "that's right" as Ali the street-corner rationalist deep-sixes the catechism. Later, rumor will have it that Herbert Muhammad is displeased by his naked manifesto; but

Blood and Reggie the chauffeur, the two Muslims physically closest to Ali, seem to encourage it. And all his religious spiels are made in their presence, to murmurs of "that's right, that's the truth."

On the way out, a black man says "I never heard such fucking shit in my life." To the sportswriters though, Ali has simply made another little boo boo. He really should watch himself.

But is it a boo boo? This sounds like mainline Muslim preaching to me, seriously intended. The thesis is that black men will never get back on their own feet until they and their women (especially their women) cease being softened by Christianity. There is no mention of getting black *women* back on their feet—quite the reverse, I suspect. But black men got to throw off this cotton candy shit and quit dreaming about an afterlife, and get it *now*.

The audience is mildly stirred or shocked or at least kept awake by this seering blast at the old religion; but it's not clear what the tots are supposed to do about it. I can't imagine that this year's crop of swingers are strung out about the Virgin Birth, or taking to crime because of the Immaculate Conception. Poking fun at these may be the only way to sell a Muslim sermon to the uncaptivated, but outside of that it serves about as much purpose as denouncing the Jolly Green Giant—unless one sees it as a symbolic rejection of femininity, an attempt to get the menfolk roused up against the old biddies who tamed them and taught them to shuffle.

What interests me is the change in Ali's style. He is so different from his public persona that it might almost be someone else speaking through him—a wiry little man with glasses perhaps. I get an uneasy feeling I'm watching a ventriloquist's dummy, with Blood behind him pulling the strings. If this is what he conceives ministers to be like, we may be in for yet another stupendous rendition: Ali the long-faced clergyman.

I gather this is one of his mosque speeches, receiving its first public airing, so it gives a useful clue to what he's been doing with his spare time. It also makes a point about his past, which I had seen up to now mostly in his father's shadow. But the blacks who are most consoled by Christianity are gentle older people like his mother, who never misses a Baptist Sunday meeting. Ali loves his mother enough to take her round and round the globe. Yet ritualistically, he must renounce her beliefs again and again. And not just renounce them, but make cruel fun of them.

So his Muslim faith has accomplished the symbolic rejection of both parents without losing their love, which is like removing a tablecloth without disturbing the dishes. If he was ever a mama's boy he isn't one now, with his swaggering he-man's religion. Yet down the hall Mrs. Clay is taping interviews on what a nice boy he is.

With Bundini at Chicago Muslim convention.

171

Has he made his parents the white boys in this fight? I keep waiting for something other than race to come between him and his God, but I don't get it today. Christianity is bad because it's white—even though Christ is black. The white folk (Matthew, Mark, Luke and John, I guess—or are they black too?) have told terrible lies about the black boy. "The same man told you who you are tell you who God are," Ali says, reverting to his name-mania. "The truth will set you free, not integration . . . name one black restaurant in Cleveland." "Burger King" shouts someone. There's one in every crowd.

It is hard to believe that the Kingdom of Heaven is literally like unto a restaurant, not to mention a beauty parlor, but Ali's vision is of the earth earthy. The whole performance is like a reverse *Green Pastures,* with the Lord telling the folk to wise up and get into real estate. Well—religions tend to wind up with real estate, so they might as well begin that way. And I'm suitably impressed with his ardor even in such a cause until an antic P.R. man called Carmine Bilotti comes up and whispers, "You know how I can get him to stop? I'll tell him you guys have a deadline."

Can this be possible? Ali is in full cry, and the audience is agog for better or worse. He can't stop now, if I know my preachers. Bilotti goes over and whispers. Ali pauses in mid-thunderclap. "A deadline? That's all folks." He stalks out abruptly, only pausing to give 100 autographs. I don't know, maybe the newsmen are right not to take him seriously.

Out in the lobby, they are talking about the real fight, which is being held between promoters grappling for Ali's carcass. Don King, the old numbers boss of Cleveland, has it for now, but if this promotion bombs as seems likely, Bob Arum of Main Bout, Inc., is in there waiting to pounce. Since King is a black man and Arum a Jew, King appears to have the inside track. But the color green is also well thought of in Ali's circles, and Arum is being kept around on tiptoe, if only to raise the bidding.

Suffocating on this mixture of godliness and gold, I decide to seek out Ali's laughing holy man, Drew Bundini Brown. In a quiet restaurant, far from the bang of cash registers, I hope to get away from Ali's diamond-studded pelt and back to his soul.

Bundini is somehow taller and rangier than he sounds. He is affable, with the slight hostility of most comics before they've won a couple of rounds off you—or of blacks who think white men are easily intimidated. "You a good writer when you let it come natural," he announces right off. Adding, "That's just a guess, I never read you." I don't know, maybe it shows.

I ask him where he lives between fights and he says something like: "Not where the egg crack, it where the bird fly. Just holler Bundini." I promise to try. Next question: "You haven't become a Muslim, have you?" (I see by his martini he hasn't, but one must start somewhere.) Bundini says, "What do you mean become? What does that word mean?" Oh, I don't know.

I quickly weary of playing straight man to this gnomic barrage, yet there is no kind of question that doesn't seem to set it off. E.g., "Would you care to talk facts?" "What do you think I have been talking? These are *real* facts." So this is the wisdom that Ali has been getting for the last few years. I can see how it suits his evasive style. If Ali has doubts of his own IQ, he can hide

out behind this smoke screen all day.

Bundini spent 12 years circling the globe as a merchant seaman and piling up wisdom like the Ancient Mariner. It is the kind of stuff that comes to you when you stare at the sea a lot. E.g., "The same water that keep you alive is the water you drown in" and also "The same cross they got in church they burn on your lawn." These sound like retreads to me, although he swears he is a fresh creation every day. I reflect that being a sage may be even tougher than being a comic, and you have to admire the way he works at it. Ali, unfortunately, requires a vitalist sage and not one of those sleepy Hindu ones who says, "Come back next year with *two* twigs," so Bundini has to be on all the time.

What I sense is a melancholy middle-aged man trying desperately to remain young for his boss, Peter Pan, so he can feed him the kind of lines Ali can use. "The smarter I get, the more lonely," he says. That's more like it. He asks me what tribe I come from and I don't have the wit to say Finn McCool and King Alfred. But he tells me I'm an African anyway, just like him. The way this works is that we are both Hebrews ("Solomon blessed your wedding") and Hebrews are Africans ("Africa is your daddy"). The main difference is that my nose, skin and hair have been further from the oven than his.

Coming from one of Ali's black claque, this is practically a peace offer. But I wonder if Ali's racism is fundamentally as benign as this? Several times Bundini says the same kind of things as Ali, but in a friendly version. He says that preachers don't feed anybody, but it doesn't seem to bother him. He probably doesn't feed too many himself. And he says that Jesus looked just like him—but "that don't mean I can't be a devil."

Everything I've heard that morning suddenly seems harmless and childlike. "Shorty sent me to see you. You know who Shorty is? God." Of all the infinite names of God, this has to be the most reassuring. But again how much of this playfulness remains in the new Ali? Bundini was his spiritual chum before he joined the Muslims, with their somber ferocity. Does his portfolio now contain a bit of both? At least he has hung onto Brown through the furnace of conversion. "I was the only one with him at the trial. . . . I saw more of him then than I see now. I was in the foxhole. Cosell was in the foxhole."

The most crowded foxhole since the Mayflower, I'm beginning to gather. In the gospel of Ali you had to have been there if you wanted to reap the coronation in Zaire and everyone has arranged it retroactively. But whatever Bundini's role then (and I'm told it was not that conspicuous), his great moment was Zaire itself when he endured the Master's mockery in the dressing room and then, weeping and wailing, urged him to his miracle.

As he sits across from me now, toying with the white man, it is hard to believe he can generate such hysteria. Maybe it's a form of voodoo possession at that. Speaking of which, he tells me there are seven people inside Ali and that he only knows three of them—the prophet, the champ and the child. The other four "just flash through." I have a feeling one of those four deserves watching.

Bundini may be a bit of a con man—in fact, legend has it that he once hocked Ali's championship belt—but his very patched-up, improvised nature is refreshing after the sharks in the lobby. He does ask me how much I'm paying for the interview, but when I offer to buy my own drink, he says, "If you was 19, I'd throw this water in your face." My feeling that Ali was keeping him on out of kindness may need revision. He not only adds a touch of Shakespearean low-life to Ali's curiously designed entourage, but also a kinky, possibly corrupt but real sense of self. At any rate, he is a trap for white writers in search of a character, and he knows it.

Outside in the lobby, the eternal buzz is about the Joe Bugner fight which is on, off, on, in Chicago, London, Cairo. At the Liston fight the buzz was Patterson, at the Patterson fight it was Paris, London, Mozambique. There is always a buzz. Right now Don King is in a tizzy because one of the P.R. men has insulted Cleveland (try it sometime). King also seems to be sore at me because I introduced myself as Mark Kram's dentist. (I thought King was just a local blowhard and I didn't catch his name.) This froth at the edges is still concealing the man in the middle, Ali himself, stalking the corridors, signing autographs, and being opaquely accessible like Chairman Mao.

So the legend swells like a blowfish even while you're watching the reality. Kilroy and Dundee tell me Ali is too nice to fight—Catholic nuns have begged him to quit. They also tell me that Vince Lombardi used to go crazy watching him box: what a football player he would have made. Or basketball player. It seems he has been witnessed picking up a basketball casually and hooking it in from mid-court. By now I am convinced that if he were three years old, he could win the Derby in a walk.

But the main thing is his niceness. The genial Kilroy can tell niceness stories from morning to night. Giving his last quarter to a drifter in Rome, buying a picture of a hungry kid just because it *was* of a hungry kid—am I being oversold? Ali's niceness is unmistakable, but is he really a candidate for sainthood? I remember his face this morning, stern as if he were in the ring, raking over the Virgin Birth. The new Ali super-celebrity can be used for many purposes, like Al Capp's shmoo, and Ali is infinitely obliging. Yet I sense two distinct camps fighting for his soul as well as his image—and each camp has a spy within Ali.

One thing is sure: if Ali decides to be a professional anti-Christian, he will be a cruel one. For Ali to fight something, he has to make fun of it, and this is as true of ideas as it is of people: and, as various nightclub comics have found, making fun of the Christian God is one of the few remaining ways of getting a rise out of people.

All this seems a continent away as he sits in the coffee shop the morning after the fight, reciting his poetry to me. I have been introduced as a poetry buff, which isn't far from true. I laugh at no man's poetry, even when it's meant to be funny. Ali's, this morning, is very gentle stuff, coming from a man whose knuckles are swollen like golf balls from his opponent's face. They are about wisdom, and how to cultivate it; they are about knowledge and death. It is as if the fight has drained his anger, and perhaps he needs fights for that and will be a wild man without them. We shall see. This morning's verses are in fact more like slogans than poems, and are simply the serious version of the comic catchphrases that made him a saleable product in the first place.

One can't hold the butterfly for long on the morning after a victory. His mind floats away, returns. Nervous autograph hounds, grinning hangers-on with some small claim on him, and just unidentified fame-sniffers tromp over you, and Ali services them all and sends them away with something.

"Why did you lie down in the ring last night?" I ask. (Ali had sunk to the canvas after knocking out Wepner, giving a brief Charlie Chaplin effect. I expected the ref to follow suit and everyone to be counted out simultaneously, by a drunken millionaire.)

"I always lay down after my victories." Eh? "My victories are not ordinary victories." He had lain down after Foreman and everything he did against Foreman is sacred. But is he really going to adopt a lying down style from now on? Anything is possible with this man.

He peers at a headline, makes out the word "victorious," says it slowly. Dundee has told me Ali is working hard on his reading and again, I am impressed by how unaffected he is about this. He is neither proud nor ashamed of his illiteracy; it's just something you work on, like a jab. Satisfied, he says he learned something from Wepner's rabbit punches. The fight is now being sewn up, put away. When I ask him if the first Frazier fight was his greatest, he says, "There were so many great ones." His filing cabinet is full. Wepner goes in under Miscellaneous.

Wallace Muhammad, Elijah's heir, turns up with the news that King Faisal has just been assassinated. Wallace is a soft-spoken, priestly fellow, the color of candle-wax and as delicate as lace, so it seems almost like an angelic message in the

176

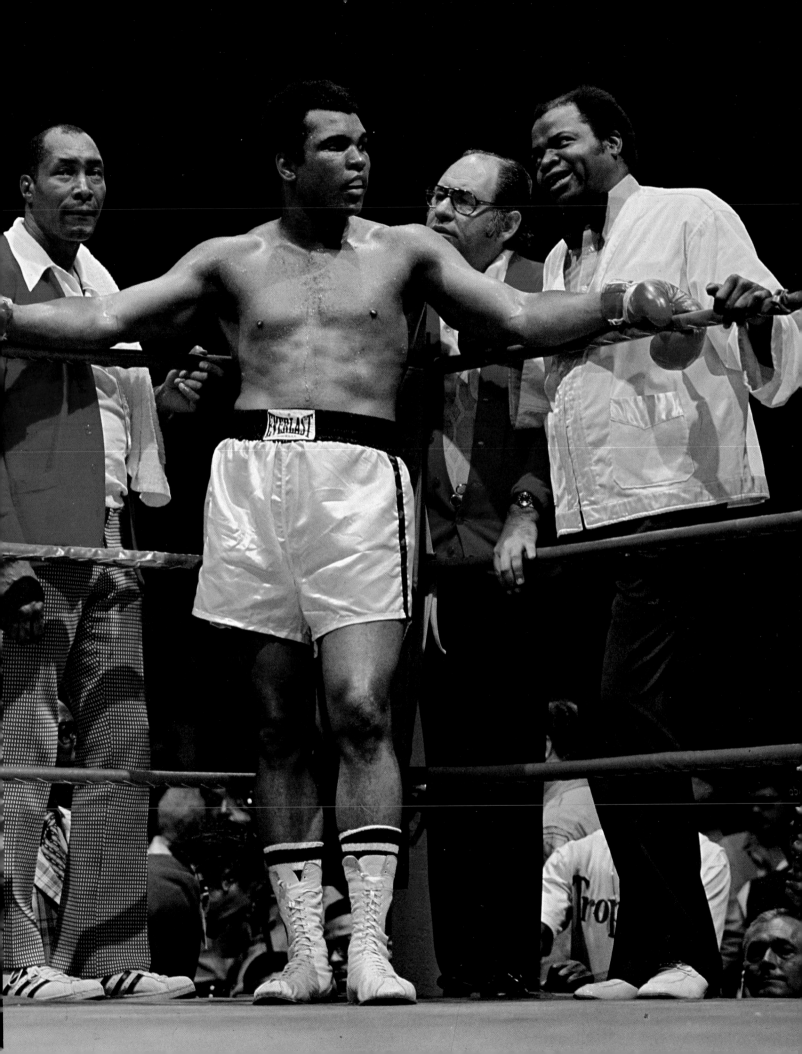

Bible. Is Ali shocked by the death of this Islamic bigwig? He doesn't show it. "He gave me a villa," he says.

Did he know Faisal? Oh yes. He visited him twice, and Faisal gave him this villa he can use anytime he wants. He has nothing else to say about him, nothing personal. He also mentions a villa in Abu Dhabi, worth half a million. A modern structure in the middle of the desert. If those villas caught fire, I sense it would hurt a lot worse than poor old Faisal's death. I ask him, apropos, if Elijah lives on anyplace. No, there is no afterlife. Only what we've got here. Bricks and mortar.

I begin to understand why the death of Malcolm X moves him so little. Dead is dead, and Ali wants no part of it; in fact, I've been warned not to tell him I have a cold. International Islam as I understand it is quite big on the afterlife, offering an extremely juicy one with girls and all, but Ali doesn't want any part of it. But I am surprised he cares so little about the politics of Faisal's murder. "It was predicted in the Bible," he says—but looking back, I'm not sure whether this means the Koran or some Muslim text I don't know.

As a leader of the Third World, Ali might be expected to care a little more about these things by now, even if only to show a vague concern. But the Third World so far is just a list of pretty names to him. These he likes to rattle off like a clever schoolboy. But for all his identification with them since Zaire, his is strictly a tourist's view; yeah, we were there for a couple of days. Yeah, I think we were there too—or was it *New* Guinea? His picture of these countries seems to be that there is a Great Man in charge, who is his friend, and lots of poor people, who are his fans.

The lessons of Zaire probably won't catch up with him until he quits boxing. At the moment, his main interest in the wretched of the earth is how much they like *him*. Otherwise he will have to wait for his instructions before he knows how he feels about Faisal: not because he is dumb, but because his present way of life absorbs all his energies. I once worked for a well-known personality, and I know how being famous saps you and throws away the skin. The man was so busy being famous that he had no time to read or to think and had to be briefed about his corn flakes. Since there was no way to grow in the mummy's bandages of fame, Bishop Sheen very admirably gave them up.

Ali's duties as Ali consist right now of making the rounds of the coffee shop, flirting decorously with everything that presents itself, kissing nameless babies—running for office on a treadmill. In Looking Glass Country, of course, you have to run twice as fast to stay in the same place, but this is a snap for the Fastest; he passes the Red Queen before God get the message and is in bed before the light go out. A hectic schedule and small wonder he doesn't keep up with the Middle East.

And talking of the Middle East: I have a brief audience with Herbert Muhammad, and it is like stepping onto the set of *Casablanca*. As he sits in the restaurant with his little court around him, he does indeed remind me of Sidney Greenstreet, and in no time we are "sir-ing" each other up hill and down glen. As in "I trust you take my meaning, sir." "Yes, I think I do, sir." Or do I dream this?

It is more a matter of atmosphere than of anything he says. Although he is Ali's business manager, and he sits for hours in the Marriott restaurant, no journalist, black or white, approaches him. Because it would be useless. All the stories they need about the next few fights are in his hat, but he doesn't give interviews. He only has ears for businessmen.

Our own conversation concerns ground rules for seeing Ali (one might as well have ground rules for seeing a sunset) and he is very pleasant and obliging when you're up close. But from a distance he and his black circle, sitting still as stones, seem a forbidding symbol of black separatism. This in a way is Herbert's role: to exchange polite conversation with the white merchant of words, but to allow no chink into his own soul. Once, before he became so dignified, he rambled with young Cassius in Miami, and Jose Torres wrote a story about it involving a prostitute, and nobody has gotten that close to him since.

Bowing my way out of the tent, I run into a much better subject: Eddie Futch, the demon manager who is in town with his man Joe Frazier. Futch is the most lucid explainer I've met in any field, and in moments he demonstrates with the help of pencil and cocktail napkin the ways to beat Ali. "Would you have managed him better than Dundee?" I ask finally. "Maybe, if he'd listened," says Futch. But of course, Ali is not a listener.

Futch and Frazier pull out, and I notice that a more buxom, smiling type of girl follows that caravan than the wispy wraiths around Ali's.

The hotel drains and the carnival moves on. The fight crowd sets off jabbering to its next appointment. The writers scatter for hockey matches, racetracks, basketball tournaments, bouncing off sports like pinballs. Lucky dogs. The hustlers go back to nickels and dimes, after their night of nights. Ali prowls the lobbies alone, by his standards. No more than two or three advisers, some stray rubberneckers—his attention scales down from groups of hundreds to groups of ten or less. I decide to watch a dismantling of Ali nation from a perch near the front desk.

Lobby sitting is good for the soul, like transcendental meditation. The mind doesn't soar, this isn't the Alps or the Lake District, but the truisms are hammered in pretty good. And one of them is that there are two black nations orbiting about Ali. One group has gone too far in the direction of integration to turn back easily. The world of boxing plays hell with your racism anyway, and it takes a conscious effort to hate somebody's color or even to notice it after a day in the gym. So Ali has picked a difficult profession to be racist in. He may need the presence of his Muslim brothers to remind him of his racist duties.

Of these, I can only report that they are just about impossible to interview if you don't have a gun. The couple I spoke to looked suspicious when I asked them their names and downright paranoid when I asked what they did for a living. No point asking them about Ali, then. Suspiciousness is their style and their essence. Concealment is a mark of manliness in the garrulous black community.

So what is a gabby fellow like Ali doing in a church like that? I have a feeling that as usual he is divided down the middle. He wants to tell everything and he wants to hide everything. His father was a talker and he has outgrown his father: yet here he is yakking away like the old man. As with his father's other hobby, sex, Ali burns to do it and to abstain from doing it at the same time. As a rule, when Ali has conflicting urges, odds are he gives in to both of them. But I do notice that he seems less candid and more programmed when the brothers are around. Walking the lobby with them he is as stone-faced as they; the very model of a strong silent Muslim. Fortunately for me these are now scattering like moths after the fight.

All day long, the autograph hounds cluster round like tugboats, giving him a chance to play King. From the armchair, in which I have dug a furrow, I wish that somebody would give him a country of his own someday: he would be terrific at helping page boys through the snow and stuff like that. Yet even at his most regal, a question that interests him will cut the crap and produce a quite startling directness. Finding these will turn out to be no easy task, though. Since I am the poetry buff, I decide to start out asking about that.

If you sit in the same place long enough, he is sure to swim past. That evening I bivouac with him at the Marriott Restaurant. I note right off that he has the world's fastest hands with a steak: zip, off with the fat. Zip, zip. What's for dessert? I wonder how he can enjoy eating as much as they say he does at that speed. So what about the poetry? Everybody has a theory about that ranging from genius to insanity. Dick Young tells me that many children write letters in verse, and someone else has said it's a sure sign of schizophrenia. So how is it with Ali? Did he write poems spontaneously as a kid?

No, not a one that he can recall. It all began as a gag after the Archie Moore fight (I believe he's got his dates wrong, but it shows how little he cares) and didn't get serious until after one of his college lectures. On that occasion, he suddenly realized that the kids were wanting something more from him than boxing, so he became a poet on the spot, the world's fastest vocation. Ali is a great spawning ground for theories, but infantile schizophrenia is one that doesn't hatch out.

I ask him who his second-favorite poet is, and he says he really doesn't have time to read that stuff. He notices a book in my lap, and there is one of those moments of luminous directness. "You read that whole thing?" he asks. I mumble that if I can write them, I guess I can read them, and he shakes his head. "I've never read one of those in my life." Since he seems really interested in what other people do with their time, I tell him it takes at least a year to write a book, with no applause at the end of the day, and a chorus of boos when it's all over, and he looks absolutely incredulous.

Turning to the other arts, I find to my surprise that he shows no interest in any of them. For instance, is it true that he plays the piano? Nope, just a few tunes that kids pick up, and a boogie-woogie bass. Umpa umpa umpa umpa. He doesn't know any chords or stuff. He even passes up the chance to boast about his singing. As a fan, he likes opera and jazz, but he doesn't cite any names and he hasn't got time for a record collection.

Hasn't got time. The theme returns again and again. To an outsider Ali's time may seem largely wasted, as he wades through his millionth crowd or roars around in his bus. And the boxing life itself consists largely of guys standing around muttering "Have you got the tape?" "No, I thought you had the tape." Yet it satiates the practitioners and it is rare to meet one with time for other interests. Even Ali, whose fans yearn that he have other interests, is awesomely indifferent to every subject one brings up.

What about painting, for instance? His daddy said he's shown some promise? If so, it's news to him. He did some drawings for *Esquire* once, but it was all in fun. My attempts to turn him into a Renaissance Man are firmly resisted, as if the world-famous braggart were almost squeamish about boasting. "Boxing gives you so much," he says—everything the Arts might have given, from the age of 12 on. Boxing also takes away so much. Reluctantly I watch my theory of Ali the artist dribble through my fingers. I ask him what he would have been if he hadn't been a boxer and he says astonishingly that he never thought about it.

"He likes to build, to create," whispers one of his followers, who may fear that Ali is giving away too much renaissance-wise. The one art that does interest him is decoration, and to confirm it, he draws me a sketch of his bus, complete with tables, chairs and bathroom. It cruises at 80 mph, he says. I've seen him showing kids around it, and he is certainly house-proud, or bus-proud. But the drawing is of no interest whatever. I ask him about his mosque-complex in Cleveland, and he says he'll certainly have a say in the design, but not the last word.

In all this, there is a totally unfeigned modesty. He wouldn't dream of telling an architect his business (I am told it is just as well. His taste is rotten). Rumors about his niceness are absolutely true. Even bitter Viet vets have been charmed by him. Making himself hateful must be his finest achievement. Because he does it so damn

well. Watching him on television a few days later, beating up on the ref again, I see something repulsive that is almost completely missing in his private manner.

My plan had been to ask him a series of questions he's never been asked before, to produce something other than the basic Ali interview. But he is ill at ease with strange questions, and either pretends not to hear them, or mumbles a monosyllable. He seems to lack confidence with people he takes to be educated, so he hides behind his prepared material. Deep down, I think he believes white people are preternaturally smart.

"Say me a poem, Ali." That's more like it. He recites several, weaving them with parables and a commentary. "Don't write this down now," he says. I am writing too slowly and he wants my full attention. "It's too bad you don't have a tape recorder." For him as for Rachaman, you don't really exist without a tape recorder. An audience of one is no audience at all. Still, he gives a full performance, and a good one.

This is what he really wants to do, and I get the idea he wishes more people would ask him to. The first poem is about different kinds of heart, whether gold or copper or wood, and how they perform: another example of his graphic sense of materials. The poem has been *imagined* line by line, so literally that there is almost no play of fancy. "If it's really clumsy, he may have written it himself," a cynic has said to me, but I don't believe that's the test. If it deals with wood or stone, it's his.

The second poem is about different kinds of wines—the wine of youth, the wine of success and so on—and the different forms of intoxication they induce. Ali is extremely interested in mental states, and

181

his profession has given him some urgent insights. E.g., "Foreman is intelligent enough for his type of fighter." One listens closely to a poet who has to bet his chin on his judgment of character.

It's a rare man who answers a question with one of his prepared lectures, but that's what Ali does now. "There's no such thing as soberness," he says. "Even for popes and Billy Graham. They have their own kinds of intoxication." His own problem is to fight for some degree of soberness, or at least a better brand of intoxication. Youth and success, he's had enough of that kind of wine; he wants something finer, more delicate now. He knows he will always be excited; what he does with that excitement is the issue.

From this he drifts into one of his favorite parables about a slave called Omar, who is put in charge of the king's treasury. (Like all children's stories, we don't know what king, what country: it might have happened yesterday, right here in Cleveland to Don King.) The king's advisers are, as is their practice, insanely jealous and they persuade the king to spy on his uppity slave. But when the slave locks himself in with the gold, and the king crouches at his knothole, His Majesty sees that the slave is merely putting on his ragged old robe, to remind himself of who he really is. The king learns humility on the spot. "You are the real treasure," he tells Omar, as the story ends.

I ask Ali if this is how he feels about his own talent and he nods. Of course. All his stories are about himself. Right now at the crest he is feverishly turning out stories about humble kings and ex-slaves.

When Ali walks the streets giving out autographs, he is being the good king in the story. "I am a humble man," he says, and I believe him, for now. If he wants something badly enough he can get it, even humility. As he gets older "being humble" could become a terrible parody. But right now he is still young enough to enjoy being a king in a fable.

Talking of which, I ask him timidly about the Muslim succession after Elijah. The *Amsterdam News* has carried rumors of power struggles; but Ali says it was an open and shut case. Allah had touched Wallace's mother's stomach when she was pregnant and that was the ball game. (Coming from a man who sneers at the Virgin Birth, this may seem a mite credulous; but there is a certain kind of earthbound miracle, of worldly mysticism, that goes down well with Islam and Ali both.) He reiterates that he has no leadership ambitions, but that he will continue to be a working minister after his ring career ends.

There he goes again, announcing his plans quite clearly. Why does nobody believe him? People ask if he's going to run for governor or movie star or prophet—but *minister?* Incredible. Unworthy of a celebrity.

I believe it's a quite genuine dream for now—which doesn't mean he'll do it. In a black community the minister is pretty hot stuff, a center of wisdom and power, not the 97-pound weakling whites envisage, and Ali may carry this image still, even if it bores his followers. And maybe he can work his intoxication off in the pulpit. I have seen him try it at the poetry reading, and the effect is like an exorcism, as the demons fly out screaming. I think again of my old boss Bishop Sheen and how he built up a larger than life self in the pulpit, and how he fought for humility, and how he finally gave up fame altogether for the sake of his soul and sought obscurity. A serious man.

I wonder if Ali will someday be faced with such a crisis, when fables about humble slaves can no longer cool the ego but become a red-hot part of it, and what he will do about it. But that can be postponed right now by boxing and more boxing and more boxing.

I have avoided this subject up to now, figuring (wrongly) that he must be sick of it. Perhaps he would like to be someday, but right now it is the air he breathes. There is more talk of the wretched Perez, and I am sorry to hear Ali's associates piling it on the ref even further. Does anybody ever tell Ali he's wrong around here? Only Herbert Muhammad it seems, and he isn't around.

Moving to less rancid matters, I am curious to learn that Ali talks with almost reverential awe of the great names of the past. Since he must know from the films that he could have whipped most of them, one must assume that he *wants* them to be great, to ennoble the profession.

Joe Louis? "He was tough. He could punch with *either* hand. And he moved like the Mummy."

Jack Johnson? "He was bad, strong and fearless. And he didn't have no Black Panther support." (I'm interested that Ali realizes this when he's comparing himself with Jack.)

Marciano? "Ah that Marciano—so much power. Bm, bm, ba, bm bm." (That's the closest I can get to the sound.) He is especially impressed by Marciano because he retired undefeated. A champion forever, something to think about.

If he were fighting these men today, he would no doubt hold them up to ridicule.

But right now it is important to set up a royal succession worthy of himself. Evidence that he may be willing to blind himself slightly in this cause is provided by Gene Kilroy, who tells me that Ali once compared Gene Tunney with Jim Corbett as quintessential dancers and presumably his own models: except that he was confusing Corbett with Errol Flynn, who played the part in a movie.

Time is up. Ali rises briskly, and leaves the restaurant as if propelled. I am reminded of my own Siamese cats who move with mysterious urgency and then stop and scratch themselves. Ali lives like a cat, and even fights like one.

I brood on my notes. Ali's poetry does not pretend to be literature—how could it, since he is totally indifferent to literature? Yet sycophants may jolly him on the point, and try to convert him into a universal genius who can do anything. So far he has resisted this admirably, and seems honestly delighted when one of his poems is praised even guardedly. Life in the ring makes one a realist in some ways.

His poems must be seen as an aspect of his ministry and as such, they are not at all bad. They are no more childish than most sermons and a good deal more sincere. One reason writers have underrated Ali's ministry is that they think of the Muslims as a rip-off. They'll even tell you that he's tired of the Muslims and would quit if he could. But even if he did, he'd still preach; he's tasted the fine wine of the pulpit, and would want more even if he had to invent his own religion. He really doesn't give a damn about poetry, "but I've done a lot of thinking. I've got it up here," he taps his forehead.

Has he? Is he really that much brighter

than the gibbering animals he claims he fights? Perhaps not, if one applies the same standards as he applies to them. A stupid fighter is rare in the top ranks, as Ali very well knows. (Off camera, he gets on better with other fighters than with any other class of human being.) But the mental adjustments of boxing are too fast for words. "Stick him, move, jab" are the most eloquent instructions he is raised on. More than that would clog the reflexes. Like higher math, boxing almost transcends language. In fact, I know a theoretical physicist who sounds exactly like a punchy prizefighter when he talks about religion and politics. "I have ideas and sometimes I put them into words," said Einstein.

Hence the lifelong questions about Joe Louis' intelligence and Ali's intelligence. When Louis troubled to speak, he made poetic connections that captivated even T. S. Eliot; yet you knew there was no point asking Joe about inflation or the role of women. His mind would have rejected the question instantly as useless to him. Such minds are not slow but too fast, geared to the here and now, the present threat. Don't let the heavy tongue mislead you.

As for Ali, people are disillusioned when they find that a *fast* tongue can be equally misleading. Unlike other fighters, Ali would like to be good at words, but his mouth is still way ahead of his brain, leading it, instructing it. The easy exchange of verbal concepts that we call intelligence is new to him right now, and I scrapped all the clever questions friends had suggested I ask him. Yet the equipment is in there if a 33-year-old semi-literate can learn how to run it. If a tongue can move fast as a jab, maybe a brain can move fast as a tongue. For the first time since Jose

Torres, the instinctual intelligence of a fighter may burst into real words.

In which case watch his fighting slip. Torres faded the moment he began translating ring language into verbal language. It was like DiMaggio thinking of the nature of curve balls or Secretariat wondering how a horse's legs really move. Words actually slow the brains of athletes, which move like lightning in their own fields. Ali might be advised to stay as dumb as he is until he retires. Yet I swear there's something going on in there, a form of thinking unchastened by books and other men's ideas, aiming only at emotional release and the big bang. The question is, is it friendly? Which of his seven souls has the franchise? Grumpy, Happy or Doc?

There is a glaze over his manner tonight which makes it impossible to tell. I'm told he has learned to manipulate writers like a grand master, and he has had a lot of practice in the last few days. I am also told that catching him alone can induce a Garbo-like shyness. I have already seen him sit so deeply silent that it looks as if he will never speak again. Only a fit of screaming can break the spell.

In all this, he is like one or two famous actors I have interviewed. They are much better observed in action. I see Ali again in the lobby that night and he is once more performing, though rather joylessly—this time for a family of autograph hounds, a timid white boy, and just the people who sprawl around lobbies like stray sections of newspaper.

Too much. No one will get all his love so long as there's another human alive. I mosey off into outer darkness. He is last seen looking for a rope to do his rope trick, whatever that is.

Running, Running

Back in New York the next day, I came jolting against his media self again like a plate glass door. Everyone has their own crotchets about him, and as they talk, the reality is replaced by the face on the tube. Ali is the sum of what people think about him; and all he can do is add to that sum, and wiggle it about as long as we're interested.

By now, I'm not sure I've really met him myself. "What's he really like?" "He's smart, isn't he? Tell me he's smart." I feel that they're asking the wrong questions and. barking up the wrong Ali, but all they have to go on is his routine with Cosell which shows him at his most artificial. Right now he is sitting with good trouper Howard, his lip practically in curlers. ("Show disdain, Ali," I can almost hear a photographer shout.) It is some days after the fight, but he is still lambasting the ref, still behaving like the roller derby. And he again drags in race, flopping and kicking. He says the Puerto Ricans should be ashamed of Perez (why?) and that he never gets a break against white fighters, as if he needed one.

"Chuvalo hit my privates for 15 rounds," he says next, which is pretty daring talk for network television. Is he losing control, or does he think he can get away with anything these days? In pursuit of his vague, tormented racism, he then makes a surprising admission. "Frazier whipped my behind fair" in the first fight. At the time, he had wanted to take a national poll on the decision; but now he's willing to concede defeat, the better to zap whitey.

Meanwhile to keep his section of the pot boiling, George Foreman takes on five palookas in one forgettable night in Toronto. The worst of it is that George tries to be funny. Like one of those Russian bears riding a bicycle, he goes through the motions of comedy without the slightest idea of why. He dances like Ali, but with a grim clumsiness; he wrestles an opponent to the floor and hits one of his cornermen, with all the melancholy of Emil Jannings imitating a rooster in *The Blue Angel*. Foreman seems obsessed with Ali since their jungle romp and wants everything he has, including his wit and charm.

189

With daughter Maryum.

To complete the route, Ali himself has flown up to Toronto to heckle, and to exhibit yet another facet of his character: which is just that, like many comedians, he has all the makings of a prize bore. He has prepared no new material for the occasion, and he grates like Jerry Lewis on a bad day. A case for the vaudeville hook all around. When Ali's stuff isn't working, he just seems obnoxious, whether he feels that way or not.

But if he is really trying to wheedle another fight with the white public, he is not getting very far. A quick check with taxi drivers and my liquor store dealer informs me that he is overwhelmingly OK with them. "Other people make up that loudmouth stuff of his," says one. "I'll bet he's really smart, you know?" says another. And a third: "What I like about him is he's nice and clean."

This last carries weight because I hear it in Miami Beach, my next port of call, and the spokesman has fled from Brooklyn to get away from black muggers, and still seems obsessed with them: yet Ali is clean with him.

Back where it all began, then: the Fifth Street Gym in Miami, a down-at-heels shrine that perfectly reflects the proprietor's character. Angelo Dundee has deliberately kept the place a boxer's workshop, as shabby and functional as an artist's studio. To a fan, it's like dying and going to heaven. For Ali, it must be like returning to one's first grade classroom, and jamming your legs contentedly under the old desk.

"This is how it used to be," says Dundee, who is already my oldest friend. Luis Sarria is anointing Ali with his magic chrism, Dr. Ferdie Pacheco is round the corner eating his lunch. This was the original crew, before life became so complicated.

Dundee is too discreet to complain about the Byzantine layers that have grown up around Ali since then, but he does say, "You asked me in Cleveland what all those guys do. I don't *know* what they do." Whatever it is, Ali seems to want a breather from it now. He has struck camp in Pennsylvania and returned to the simple life. Members of the entourage have been requested not to follow.

I take this to be a fresh turn in his post-Zaire personality. He has been getting too frantic, acting too hard, spinning out of control. He has been saying everything that comes into his head, a terrifying load. Against Wepner he used language unbecoming a Muslim, and afterwards he lost his delicate hold on humor. He never really smiled in Cleveland, only mugged. The angry devils were pounding too hard. So, like a drunken driver he has pulled over to the side of the road.

He trains quietly today and without hysterics. His next opponent is one Ron Lyle, nothing to get excited about, but Ali is not even giving it the routine dementia; he has told Cosell that all that racist talk belongs back in the sixties, flabbergasting your observer one more time. When he leaves the ring today, he seems like a different guy from the star-studded robot I half-met in Cleveland. He has shed his polychrome glaze and he looks at one directly without his eyes skittering off in the corners. He really smiles without that tightness around the mouth that means he's faking it.

Back in the rubdown room, which is the size of a cigar box, we solemnly shake hands (I never know what the man will do next) and chat about the Foreman fiasco in Toronto. The conversation is a fair sample of Looking Glass logic, which is entirely Ali's servant. "Foreman looked good for his weight," begins Ali. "He'd been eating. Any fighter in the world would have trouble in that condition."

He stresses the superhuman difficulty of knocking out five people, *any* five people, including your mother-in-law, in one evening, and says that the public is "hypocritical" about Foreman. "He's only lost once and they're calling him a bum." Then he does a back flip. "I went up there to learn something, but he didn't show me nothing. He was looking bad for me. *Foreman* is hypocritical." (My italics.)

So Foreman was looking good and bad at the same time, depending on what point you're making. I am getting entirely used to this. I ask him how he rates Foreman as a comic dancer. "He went through the motions," he says.

Foreman may be obsessed by him, but he isn't obsessed by Foreman. He can drop the subject any time. Jimmy Ellis comes squeezing into the room and they rap with each other like the old friends they are. Ellis is a boyish man, ready to laugh at a moment's notice, and Ali picks up the mood right away yakking back and forth, as if they were still a couple of scrawny 14-year-olds from Louisville hitching a ride to the TV show called "Tomorrow's Champ" on which they fought each other. Twenty years ago, imagine. Altogether, Ali and Ellis fought twice as amateurs, splitting the honors, and Ali talks of fighting him one more time, as if to settle it once and for all. (Alas, Ali has already desensitized Ellis

once as a pro, and can do so to infinity, but he'd like to give his old friend a payday.) Ellis tells me on the side that Ali hasn't changed a wink since the old days—not to friends, anyway. "He always talked," he says.

The conversation turns to children, and Ali says, "If you got a daughter, you pay." The gist is that we "jack up" other people's daughters, but if we found someone else doing that to ours, we'd go bananas. Again he's picking at that scab. Women. But it's a lighthearted conversation, even if it doesn't sound it, and for a while Ali could be an average guy spitballing with friends. He has shaken out his public self, and I see what sweet fun it must have been in the old days. Outside on the phone Dundee is saying, "You want a medium-rare fighter, I'll get you a medium-rare fighter." And on the walls, the photos of Kid Chocolate and Ken Oberlin look down benignly on a new generation of aspiring pugs.

There are two nagging reminders that Ali's public self can run but it can't hide, in the form of two white acolytes who sing his praises ceaselessly like the cherubim in the heavenly choir. One of them makes sure I take down his name (I take it down) and proceeds to break out a new batch of niceness stories about Ali, which he tells in a normal voice a few feet from Ali's head. I have noticed this phenomenon before— people talking about Ali as if he wasn't there. He obligingly seems to tune out until the flattery runs down.

Meanwhile, Acolyte Two is telling the champ what a great movie his life story would make, with him in the starring role. "What a great actor you'd be," burbles the lad. This is just fresh cream for Ali's whisk-

Ali and Belinda with the brood.

ers—but are they never allowed to dry? Ass-kisser One tells me that Ali once outran a quarter horse for a short distance. "That's right," says Ali, "for a short distance." So the scoundrel has been listening all along.

At some point a chap comes in and announces he is a law officer from Dade County, which is certainly what he looks like, and that he has some papers to serve on Ali. "I don't want 'em," says the champ, and the law officer grins. "I missed you at the banquet," he says.

The papers concern Tony Perez' suit for $21 million against Ali, and the champ hands them gravely to the press (Bob Lipsyte and me). I note from them that Ali is alleged to have called Perez a white motherfucker during the fight, along with Wepner. Somehow obscenity doesn't seem right for Ali: it reminds me of the brain disease that makes nice old ladies swear uncontrollably. Mrs. Clay's little boy learned the street words but not the music. Anyway it all seems a million miles away from this musty little rubdown room where Ali the cat smiles and smiles.

A.K. One completes his morning's labors by assuring me that Ali is wiser than any of the professors at Miami University. It sounds possible. Ali picks up the cue and gives us a few lines from his lecture on child-rearing. Punctuality, concentration and charity must all be taught in the early years—it's a fine time to be telling me this *now*. The spontaneity with Ellis seems to have been switched off under this hail of praise.

Talking of children, Ali's own are in town with their mother Belinda, and little Muhammad Ibn (which means son of, or junior) Ali puts in an appearance at the

193

gym. He's a cheery little guy, very much at ease with his father. As he perches on the old man's chest, Ali says, "He's branded for life, but he don't know it." Considering who branded him, and how Ali struggled against his own father's name, it seems strangely arrogant of Ali to have made his own son a junior. But whether Junior lives to loathe his father's legend or to glory in it, he certainly doesn't seem branded right now. Ali is as natural and fatherly with him as he was artificial and media-fatherly with the kids in Cleveland. After a while little Muhammad runs out and begins punching the heavy bag, with a nice overhand stroke, without a thought to the burdens of fame.

The second question everybody asks about Ali, after they've inquired about his brains is, what is his wife like? But things are arranged so that you will never know. Belinda was raised a strict Muslim and her character is concealed, as by a veil. A close friend tells me that she can loosen up and be pretty funny; or then again, she can be chilly and dignified. But it's not for the press to say.

The only real clue to Belinda, outside of four clear-eyed children, is her effect on Ali. When she is around, he is observed to train harder and behave himself, like most husbands; but more to the point, he is much easier to talk to.

It's good to see Ali in this setting. He may be a complicated man, but at least one of his seven souls is simple. I don't know, perhaps they all are.

Before I see him again, I check in again with Ferdie Pacheco, the most interesting member of Ali nation. Pacheco looks like a cynical ship's doctor who cuts off your leg in a thunderstorm and saves the day. In real life he has a slum practice in the ghetto, in an office full of bullet holes, but the nice thing is, you would never peg him for a saint. If he ran a numbers racket down there, he wouldn't have to change his style a hair.

During the course of a long, funny evening, Pacheco gives me one small hint as to why this is so. A doctor working the corner in a fight is not like a normal doctor, he says. He must keep his man fighting at all costs—even with a broken jaw, as in the Norton fight (yes, the jaw *was* broken by the second round, he says); he must sit by while trainers stuff anticoagulants into cuts, in a way that will undoubtedly cause scar tissue; he must in short forget his usual instincts until after the fight, when he becomes once more a healer.

There is nothing wrong with this. Pacheco informed Ali his jaw was broken and that was all he could do. If he became a nag about little things like that, Ali would simply get himself another doctor. But the ambiguity has perhaps rendered Pacheco less glib with moral judgments than most people, and has fortified his shaded, Joseph Conrad approach to mankind.

It would be pleasant to linger on Pacheco, with his stable of classic cars—including a former Mexican president's open-top Packard, which he drove me around town in—and his professional cartooning and a dozen other improbabilities, but duty presses. Some other time perhaps.

Pacheco takes a doctor's-eye view of Ali, as one of his 2,000 or so black patients, so you get a more life-size view than you get from the flack-persons. He tells me Ali really does have a sense of humor when he isn't "being funny." For instance, on seeing a shack in Africa with 12 cars out front, he says, "Must be a nigger"—a nice twist of self-parody, since Ali is a car maniac himself. It is always that kind of humor, fast, ethnic and curiously unsuited for media use.

All in all, Pacheco seems sincerely impressed with Ali—which is reassuring, since he works the corners for nothing and is free to speak. He says that Ali is the most unchanging character he knows; that whatever convulsions may occur under the surface, the façade remains serene. Even in defeat he is stoically cheerful. After the Norton

fight, he wound up consoling his handlers through his broken jaw; he'd put others in the hospital, and now it was his turn.

On the other hand, he refused to be hospitalized after the Frazier fight, because he was afraid word would get out. He accepts the inevitable, but only when it can be proved.

I ask Pacheco why Ali broke camp in the Poconos to come down here (Miami in late April is a special taste) and Pacheco answers with an incident. It seems a few days before, his Cuban cook had come in to announce a big black stranger in the kitchen. That must be some other-worldly cook, because the stranger was Ali, by himself for once, and eager to fool around with Pacheco's cars.

In other words, he wants to be a kid again: to shed all his crazy roles, martyr, king, preacher, and jazz around with old cars, his first love. You know he means it, because he doesn't bring a single reporter

or cameraman. And Miami helps him to simplify in other ways. Up north, his inability to say no creates situations of nerve-wracking complexity. Even his hangers-on have hangers-on by now. One week, a stranger will show up at the camp, and by the next he will be on the staff and complaining about *other* strangers showing up. It is like a political campaign: everyone wants to pull up the gangplank once he's on board.

Ali escapes to Uncle Angelo's playpen to be himself. Yet even here, complications start brewing in no time. Not just the lily-white groupies of this morning, but requests for appearances and exhibitions that send him spinning up and down Florida, and will make this place unendurable too. Everywhere he goes this happens—because part of him insists on it. Tomorrow he is due to launch a supermarket in Orlando and then to do some sparring in Daytona Beach. So I thank Dr. Pacheco for a fine evening, which included watching his wife dance with Jose Melendez and other non-Ali-related activities and make plans to rendezvous with my subject in Daytona. I see by my notes that Pacheco has compared Ali's world with *Alice in Wonderland*. Oh, well.

The next scene finds me slumped in the shadows of Ali's bedroom in Daytona, disguised as a friendly journalist. To follow Ali is to share his contexts.

At the moment he is lying naked under a sheet watching "Candid Camera" and shushing some people who are talking. (Like many athletes, he enjoys being naked and strips down at every opportunity.) He is impassive, but there isn't much to laugh

at. The show fades out and is replaced by the seven o'clock news. The rout is on in Vietnam, and Ali seems interested. After all, this war has made him a national issue, so it's time he learned something about it.

"Have they captured the chief city yet?" Saigon is on the brink it seems, but not yet fallen.

"Why couldn't we beat the North Vietnamese?" he asks. "Is it the numbers?"

Everybody chimes in with a theory, which taken in sum add up to all the theories there are. Nobody goes so far as to say it was because Ali wasn't there. But Ali returns to his numbers notion. "It's like swatting flies. You get tired and run." Then after a moment, he adds that maybe the trouble was getting our military supplies that far. They wouldn't have licked us in California. It is as if he has just heard about the war that caused him so much grief, and is slowly doping it out.

The talk turns to ghetto housing, and again he approaches it with fresh interest, as if for the first time. His voice is, as usual, low, aimed at the guy next to him, but I gather he is saying that public housing lacks the profit motive, presumably as opposed to Muslim housing. But all these problems come down to people like us sitting in rooms, he says, talking, not able to do anything much. Coming from a man who set the country on its ear for three years, this is a somber thought. But that's enough of this heavy stuff for now; it's time to get out to the local cow palace and do some dancing. He runs for the bathroom giggling, for fear any girls might pass through.

A local dignitary drives us out to the high school stadium, where Ali is due to exhibit. In transit, Ali's style is to ask a stream of polite questions about the town and its environs—is there much farmland? How long is this strip anyway?—like a foreign official jollying his hosts. If he takes in the answers, he must be a very well informed man by now. But the questions lead nowhere, and are not followed up. Every town is a foreign country to Ali now. He is an ambassador at large even in his own bedroom.

There is one bright moment. Ali asks, "Do the girls around here play at night?" and the dignitary answers, "Oh yes, they play tennis all the time."

A girl pokes her head in the bus to say that she hates boxing but loves Ali. Later in the evening he will say that there are folks who hate boxing and love Ali. Nothing is wasted. Ali changes inside the bus while the crowd surges and pounds outside, like the sea. In this small town, 1,000 miles from Madison Avenue, they are chanting for Howard Cosell.

It seems like an average evening. Enterprising fans try to wriggle onto the bus, and are treated as courteously as possible. Ali's court photographer Howard Bingham actually takes pictures for them with their own cameras, and otherwise serves as Ali's curator. Bingham is, by vote, the nicest guy in Ali's court, so it's reassuring to know that he is always there, when the hustlers have fled. Tonight he shows that he is a whiz at siphoning the public in and out, so that everyone gets a piece of the Old Master without eating him alive, and he is an essential part of the publicity machinery. A lot of the small-change good will that Ali leaves behind is Bingham's doing.

Ali's sparring partners tonight are genuine pure-grade stiffs, so he gets a chance to strut his whole repertoire, including a very funny imitation of George Foreman imitating him. Against guys like Wepner, he has business to attend to which cramps his comedy, but here he can satirize the very soul of boxing. He is a first-rate physical comedian and could surely make it with the Harlem Globetrotters if he so wished. The small crowd laughs and claps, except for a couple of grim white men from an earlier era, whose arms are folded like grill-work.

Ali also does his fetal routine, crouching behind his arms and letting himself be hit. "Show me somethin', show me somethin'." He chants litanously. And then, "You ain't got nothin', you ain't got nothin'." And finally, to the crowd, "He's gettin' tired, he's gettin' tired. He's mine, he's mine."

No press conference would be com-

With Bundini (back to camera) at Fifth Street gym.

201

plete without this enactment, and it looks more grotesque every time I see it. "It's my new style," he explains. But it must be murder on his kidneys, which stick out from ambush and are belted at will. And it lacks all the proud elegance of his old style. Why does he do it on a night like this, when he has come to show off?

Well, he believes in this style and proclaims it with religious passion, and if it really accomplished the miracle of Zaire, he has reason to. A friend of mine versed in behavioral science tells me that it is also the pose of the classical masochist, but this could just be a quaint coincidence: boxing styles replicate all kinds of bizarre emotions, but they aren't chosen for that.

However it is a good enough theory to kick around on a dank night in Daytona. Ali has parodied so much of human experience—why not masochism? And what use is a mystery man if you can't make up stories about him? Anyway, it seems that the classical masochist is invariably the victim of child abuse, *real or imaginary*. (*What happened in those first 12 years in Louisville?*) Masochism is, in root, a rather spunky, noble response to such abuse. Instead of collapsing, the victim says in effect—go ahead and hit me. "Show me something." Your tormentor must then either kill you or give up, defeated. "It's like swatting flies. You get tired and run."

The masochist needs a strong core of self-belief to survive at all, and he keeps himself going with dreams of ultimate conquest and transcendence, of being the greatest; but something tells him that daddy or whoever will always be there to thwart him. So he makes the beating its own re-

ward; the defeat is his victory, and martyrdom is his crown.

This could be one of Ali's seven souls, but if so he has another one to match it and round out the drama, because he is not only the victim but the executioner. His favorite role in fighting and life is the 97-pound weakling who comes back: hence his popularity with intellectuals. But like a writer he can pluck from his own psyche a coward, a bully or whatever he likes. Right now he may be acting out some dim memory or forgotten dream. "You ain't got nothin'." My old man could hit harder than that. "He's tired, he's tired. He's *mine.*"

Anyway, this is a long way away from the clown capering above my head right now, spraying sweat on the onlookers. "I like your town and I like your style, but your equipment's so bad, I won't be back for a while." He announces that no heavyweight champion has ever fought without headgear in front of so few people paying so little money, and everybody laughs. No one, outside of the cast-iron Aryans, is mad at Ali. Little white bigwigs are busting their britches for his attention, and clamoring to have their picture taken with him.

Surely he has won now? Or can a masochist ever win? One's mind drifts to President Nixon. No, that's ridiculous. This is a very different Capricorn.

Ali likes to relax after a fight, even a silly one. Now he sits slumped in the Daytona airport shooting the breeze with the world at large. Any old subject will do. We settle on cigars. What the hell? It could be azaleas or men's suits. That's how it goes when you talk to royalty. "Do they bother you?" I ask. (His Muslim attendants won't allow them within 100 feet of him.) "Nah. They bother *you,* though. Except you don't inhale them do you? . . . Chris and Angelo Dundee, I call them Heckle and Jeckle with all that cigar smoke." He approaches every subject like a tourist. While we are talking, various old men scuffle for the seat next to him, as if it were Santa's lap. The first view of a celebrity is like first love: it's never the same again. Most of the time, though, the prize seat is occupied by foxes, lithe as fashion models, who follow each other in mysterious rotation.

Camp breaks up the next day and Ali resumes his catlike wanderings—Mississippi, Louisville for the Derby, who knows what after that. The last day in Miami is show biz as usual. John Hess, a karate champion, is on hand for a little agitating and Ali falls to with a will. In amongst sparring three rounds with Ellis and three with another guy, he finds time to shake his fist at Hess, and threaten to come and get him. "After I whup you, they won't call me Ali. They'll call me *Bruce* Lee."

Hess is a quiet fellow and even Dundee's sly prompting can't get him to scream back. But he does agree to, go one round with Ali (agree hell, he's brought his uniform) and the result, as planned, is just enough to whet the appetite. Ali seems to be just as good at dodging feet as he is at dodging fists, but it's hard to tell because Hess, futzing around in his jammies, is apparently trying to miss him anyway.

Afterwards, Ali shouts taunts over his dressing room wall, and rushes out a few times to resume battle. Even a hardened observer cannot be absolutely certain he isn't serious—because, as always, he is a *little* bit serious. Each time, the obliging Bingham rushes over in mock alarm to break things up, then scurries off laughing. Between outbursts, Ali says, "Did the press get that?" (Yes, boss.) Then he talks about how he would like to add karate to his accomplishments, so he'd be "two champions," and in no time he is outlining his tactics for the forthcoming fight. "It's something new in my mind," he says. Clearly, just being heavyweight champion is no longer enough, and he is beginning to thresh around for more.

Outside, Hess seems winded, if only by the psychological blitzkrieg. He confides to the bystanders that Ali would be awfully hard to beat over 15 rounds. "I'd try to hit him in the neck," he says—but he's not sure he could hurt a man in such great condition as Ali. "He's awfully strong," Hess mutters. Later, for public attribution, he will sound more confident; but right now he is recovering from Ali's personality.

Ali wraps it up. "It comes down to guts," says the old tactician. "I'm nervous about him and he's nervous about me. But he's heard more about me than I have about him."

I knew that Ali has a thousand ways to psych you but I hadn't quite realized how he uses his sheer celebrity to beat you. That's why Hess was sweating out there. He'd never encountered so much crazy fame before.

Ali is lying face down, his favorite talking position. The other half of the press (Lipsyte) has pulled out for New York, and we are alone, except for a roomful of people.

He turns to me with the friendliest

207

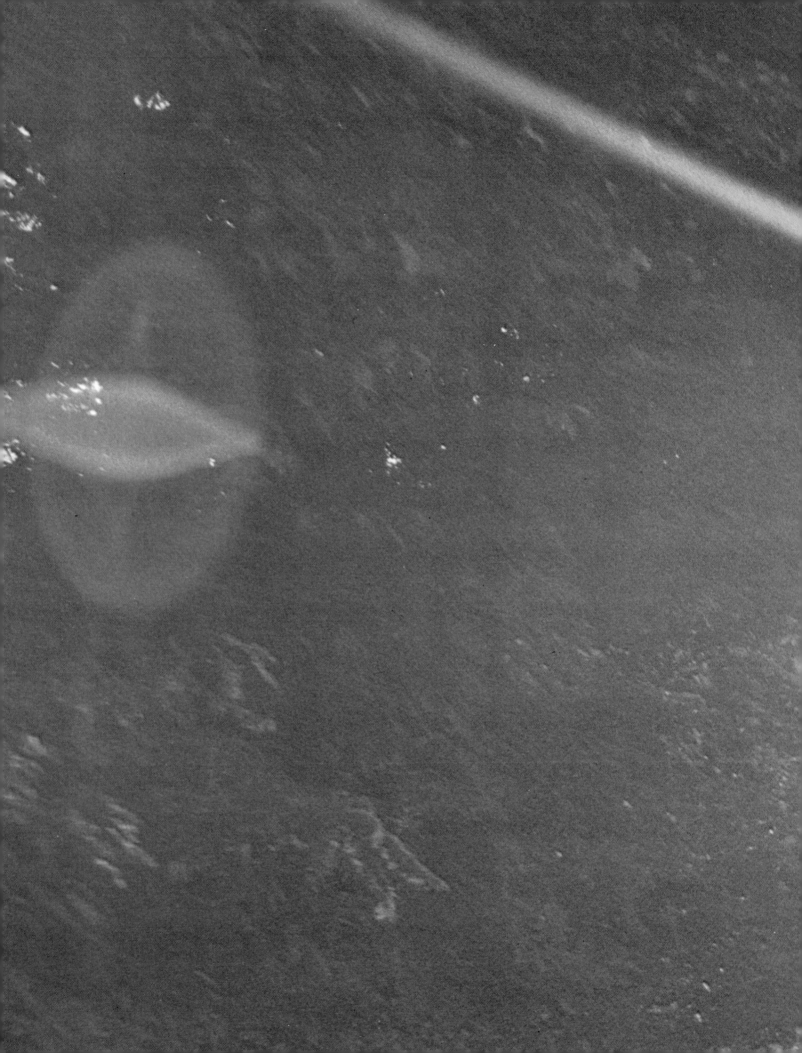

expression I have yet seen—downright comradely. "A couple of guys told me not to talk to you too much. It ain't illegal or nothin', but they told me not to."

The guys in question must be the perpetrators of his upcoming autobiography, which is slowly being ground out by a former editor of *Elijah Speaks.*

"Why do you suppose they're so nervous?" say I.

He laughs. "Everybody's nervous. Coz they're afraid the other guy may be better. You may be as good as my guy, you may be better." He talks about the nature of competition in general, and I suddenly realize it is a real conversation and not a series of polite questions or a scrap of a sermon. My rivals have given us something to talk about.

He says he'd like everyone to write about him, and I'm sure he would: Nabokov, Dear Abby, everybody. I tell him I'll just have to make up a lot of crazy lies about him, and he laughs and says, "Right!" (When more honest countenances are made, Sheed will wear one.) We discuss briefly the character of his autobiographer (sterling) and agree that, just as an abstract proposition, a good book from me would be better than a bad one. "Right!" When there is a subject in hand, an enterprise, his face focuses and his mind seems twice as quick. He would obviously like to talk all day about not talking. But on the whole, I prefer to hear him talk to non-writers. I don't believe he is ever quite himself with writers: it is always a game, always an attempt to plant his legend. The best of Ali is overheard.

210

I see him one more time, by blind chance, at the Miami airport. I swear the man bi-locates.

"What you doing, spying on me?" he says smiling.

I hold a finger to my lips. The non-talking game breaks him up completely.

I don't know what he's doing at the airport. It's years since he had to buy his own tickets. So I guess he just wants to mix with his people for a minute. For once, though, nobody seems to recognize him, which leaves him at a loss. And I suddenly remember the question I wanted to ask concerning the depth of his religious belief. "Tell me about the Muslim spaceship, Ali," I ask.

"Well," he pauses. "I hear a lot of things about that. Some folks say it's been up there for 30 years, and all kinds of stuff like that. But I don't know." Another pause. "Wallace Muhammad says all that spooky stuff is out."

At the exit, he turns and gives an apologetic wave. Saying goodbye to a writer is such sweet sorrow. He returns, not to the black part of Miami where he spent his first ardent days as a Muslim, but to the Fontainebleau, home of boiled white flesh. This is known as beating whitey at his own game. I am outside the looking glass again, and must put all the toys back in their boxes—Angelo Dundee, Ferdie Pacheco, Sarria the masseur: every one of them worth a book. But who would read it, so long as we've got celebrities?

Anyway, if I can't get back into Wonderland, Las Vegas will do. And that's where we're going next.

The White Rabbit Wraps Up the Case

Nobody can really dominate Las Vegas, not even the Old Thug, because its mind is elsewhere. This was my first encounter with the machines which greet you at the airport and hog the lobby and try to get into your room, and I was as overwhelmed by them as any old man with orange hair.

The machines run the town, with a little help from the croupiers, and in what follows it helps to picture them banging away round the clock, pretty as paint, always giving a little less than they promise.

Celebrities dash themselves against Vegas in endless waves, and the tourists dash themselves against the celebrities, and within a couple of days even Wilt Chamberlain can walk the casino unnoticed. It is the best possible cure for fame-fever: you see so many stars that Muhammad Ali becomes just another pretty face. Gambling is what the place is about—an activity so intense that lesser emotions like jock-sniffing and fame-sucking are smartly burned away.

Ali's entourage may hit a town like Cleveland like a black fist, but here they are lost in the carnival. And Ali himself seems even more relaxed, in the eye of the fame hurricane, than he did in Miami. Spotting your reporter, disguised as a future Nobel Prize winner, he gives me the athlete's hand slap. "Hey, old man."

"I'm not talking to you," I say severely. He grins and shakes his head, and mutters something that might possibly be "ah shucks." Not being able to talk to somebody is still a new experience for him, and every time he spots me, he throws me a conspiratorial grin. It is like a beautiful friendship between two trappist monks. But the fact is that Ali has been over-interrogated by now. He has answered every question that he's ever going to answer someplace or other, and the last thing he needs is more questions. I could always send some up by room service. But old reporters tell me that I'll find the answers in back numbers of *Ebony*. I would even say that questions bring out the dullest side of his character.

His behavior is much more creative and revealing than anything that goes on in his conscious mind.

What Hitchcock calls the McGuffin, or story point, of this trip is the Ron Lyle fight. Hitchcock believes that, although his movies are about horror, you have to have a story, however silly; so it goes with Ali's promotions: the subject is hoopla, but you have to have a fight.

I am here to see him go another round with the Bitch Goddess: and as usual I have no idea what tactics he will use. His McGuffin is not necessarily my McGuffin. I also want to check out Ali's touring company, which I follow like a serial or moveable novel. Right off, I run into Cassius Clay, Sr. dressed to the nines in a green jump suit singing "I did it my way" at the end of the Tropicana bar. Pretty damn well, too. More pathos than the Thug. Up in the press room, Bundini Brown announces his presence by walking slowly around the joint like a model at a fashion show. He will clearly

be available for interviews. Dundee and Pacheco wander through, like an old dream, or a class reunion. One could easily become addicted to this, as people do to chasing the circus. Pacheco startles me by mentioning the kidnapping of the Mayaguez by the Cambodians. It is the first and last mention of the outside world by any of Ali's immediate circle that week.

There is a mood of Indian summer about this fight. Lyle is the last patsy Ali can afford to take on before facing reality in the form of a contender. Then the championship can go just like that, and probably for good. One night soon Ali will reach into his bag and find it empty; call on a reflex and find it missing. However good a fighter may look in training, he only knows when the bell rings whether he's still got it—a nerve-wracking condition for a virtuoso. (Imagine how your favorite violinist would feel.)

Therefore, Ali's nervous system is always a fresh story. But for Lyle he seems ominously (or reassuringly) calm. Larry Holmes, a former sparring partner who's beginning to go places on his own, says that Ali is only the minimum nervous. "He's in great shape. You can tell by how much he's talking. Talking really takes it out of you," says Holmes. (Who adds, "I love him, but I'd like that championship.")

Ali seems to have made peace with his new super-self after the agitations of Cleveland. And he seems to have made other kinds of peace as well. I find his wife Belinda in the bedroom suite chatting merrily with his extended family of foxes. In fact somebody asks her to pose with them for a group photo with foxes. Belinda's face is much more open and responsive than I'd been led to suppose, and she seems to be inching out of the Muslim closet. But she is still guardedly polite with strangers, if I'm anything to go by.

The kingfish lies sprawled on the bed (he is the world's champion sprawler, resting on the base of his spine even in an upright chair) while the girls chatter like three little maids from school—or like Mrs. Clay and her friends. "When you leaving, where you going?" And from Belinda, "I never met a good Gemini yet." Mrs. Clay herself passes through like someone looking for an umbrella, and every kind of group picture is taken. Even the gloomy Rachaman unbends in this family atmosphere, and actually embraces a white man.

Ali's domestic arrangements are beyond anybody's ken, but everybody seems to be happy right now. Shirley MacLaine, who happens along, asks why such a, well, easygoing fellow should be so severe about things like nudity in movies, and he gives her some sort of a prim answer about theatricals, but in fact the contradiction goes deep into his nature. He wants to be a saint and he wants to squeeze life until the juice runs, and it is hard to combine these two objectives. "Do you mean he's a hypocrite?" asks Shirley. No, not exactly. Whether he is breaking up a crap game among his staff or flirting with a sister, he means every word of it. He is sequentially sincere.

Right now, in his regal sprawl, he seems somehow outside of the scene. Having composed a situation, he steps away from it like a painter. Somebody is pitching him a deal about bicentennial medallions, and he is listening in that abstracted way of his. Is he taking a bigger hand in his own business life these days, or is he just being polite? At times like this, his face

make Joe Louis' seem Parisianly expressive.

Before the press is shooed out, he has a few words with Belinda, and I can only report that he sounds just like a husband. How many of Bundini's seven souls theory does that make?

Next shot. A TV interview with someone *other* than Howard Cosell. In fact he is talking to a picture of Tom Snyder beamed from New York or wherever they keep Tom Snyders. The setting is a sun-scorched patio in Ali's compound and the live audience consists of some pretty girls and Rachaman and me (disguised as an assistant cameraman), plus the girls in Ali's suite who peep through the curtain and titter, adding a sultry harem effect. The compound is guarded, but the guards change so often that they don't know who to keep out, so you just march in with the next camera crew (there's one along every five minutes).

What the camera does not show today is that Ali is playing direct to the patio audience, flirting with the girls and ranting, or not ranting, for Rachaman. His spirits are absolutely unquenchable, even though the fight is next night. He opens with a finger exercise in boasting: he expects to be the first fighter on the moon—where, I guess, he could really float. Hymn no. 73. While waiting for the moon to put up the money, he wants to fight in the Pyramids and the Roman Collosseum, which they're going to rebuild just for him. In return, he plans to ride in on a chariot "in ma Ben Hur uniform." "I do make things exciting, don't I?" he murmurs during the break.

Today the dark brooding side cannot be roused any way, even though Rachaman is rooting his heart out. Snyder asks him about the white power structure, and he gives us the current Muslim line We've got to look to our own faults, which always turn out to be the same as the other guys' anyway. The fact is that blacks are at the mercy of the white power structure for money and jobs so there's no use getting mad at it. What would happen if the balance of power were reversed is not stated: but if their faults are exactly the same as ours, white folks better start learning to dance.

Meanwhile, Brother Rachaman is shouting "preach" from the sidelines, in an agony of appeal. Ali obliges with his rigamarole about names. "You know Rodriguez is Cuban, you know Goldstein is Jewish." "Preach," shouts Rachaman. But the preacher is just going through the motions. Somebody should have told him by now that Jews were sometimes forced to take other people's names too. But who wants to argue with a parrot?

The next topic really gladdens Ali's heart—and maybe has been gladenning it all along. He has been asked to speak at Harvard University on commencement day, and is in humble awe of the invitation. "The world's greatest university with the world's wisest minds" he calls that old Yankee institution. So what is he planning to talk about up there? "Life's intoxications," he says—the same lecture he's given me as a red-hot exclusive in Cleveland.

He quotes from it now, and as usual his voice changes, like a child reading aloud, and he even pronounces words slightly different, dressing them up in their Sunday best. I understand now why his preaching sounds wooden: it has to. He dwells on the intoxication of youth—when you're young, they whip you and you do it again and again, he says. It's that same old scene,

"show me somethin', you ain't got nothin'." While the flies and butterflies keep coming. "Beautiful," says Rachaman. Ali pauses to tell Snyder what a good show he's running, and Rachaman says fervently, "You make it a good show."

One marvels at the mix of unsophistication and wisdom that makes him want to take this stuff to Harvard. If he tried to talk their language, he would be mediocre; but these lectures are a distillation of his own strange mind and have their value.

He reads a little poem about love which includes a good word for Christ. Maybe the Muslim line has changed on that too. Christians make pretty good money. Anyway, Ali feels so good the chuckles come out like bubbles. Just look at the good-looking sisters in the audience, for instance. The camera swings round to discover Sheed in a bevy of foxes. "How can I lose with the stuff *I* use," crows Ali, rolling his eyes wickedly. Since this is on national television, I assume it is a policy statement and that the penitential season is over. Writers have been covering up his enormous interest in girls out of respect for the other Ali, the holy man; but his exuberance is too great to contain. He blows the story himself.

If Ali is an enigma, it is not because he hides things but because he shows so many of them and they are all different. The more you understand him today the less you will tomorrow. So catch him now, like a cat, purring and licking his whiskers; next week he will be in the desert fasting and scourging himself. Like St. Thérèse of Lisieux, he chooses everything.

Perhaps emboldened by the unbuttoned atmosphere, Snyder asks stutteringly

how Ali feels about, er, sleeping with one's wife before a fight. Ali answers roguishly that as to sleeping with your wife and all that, he really can't say because (pause) "it's none of your business." ("Good answer, that's a good answer," says Rachaman, looking round for confirmation.)

Now as for Women's Lib, it isn't high on his list of interests. He segues into some idle feminist-baiting (Who they name hurricanes after? Why they call it a mansion not a womansion, etc.) just for fun. Even on a good day, he can't help agitating. Then suddenly the words turn more serious, even if the speaker doesn't. Women should look up to men in every way, he says. Black women in particular have been liberated too long. They've been too far away from the man.

We are back to mainline Muslim teaching, even in the goofy euphoria of Vegas. If the demoralized black man is ever to return to his family and civilization, he must come back as king. He ain't ever coming back to a liberated woman. I glance over at the window where the girls are peeping and smiling, and presumably talking about hairdos and recipes. And I marvel again at how the social activists have clasped this man Ali to their bosoms.

Once more, it seems, he has rounded on his most ardent followers and told them to get lost. Yet, who knows, someday he may lead them again in another crusade. Who can say what side he'll turn up on in ten years' time? And you never know when a martyr like Ali will come in handy.

Anyway, he is too skittish today for such heavy thoughts. Even his views on women are delivered lightly, to the approving growls of Rachaman. In this mood he can refer to angels as white bitches during a commercial break and the starkest nun wouldn't take offense. He retires to his little nest where the roses bloom and I go back to find out how the writers are doing at the gaming tables. These guys are so Ali-logged by now that he can't *give* away all the interviews that gurgle within him. "More Ali bullshit" they call it. They'd rather lose their money at blackjack.

It seems that around every corner in the Tropicana, somebody is giving a press conference. ("I'm holding mine over here," pipes Dundee, and races off down the corridor.) I look in on the last of George Foreman's, which he conducts in a curious shuffle, as if it was part of his gym work. For sheer sparkle and variety, I'd prefer President Ford, but he does say a couple of interesting things.

Apropos of Ali's new hands-over-the-head style, Foreman suggests that what Ali is really saying is, "Oh God, don't let them kill me." Not a bad piece of depth analysis for Big George. He adds that Ali has since turned down seven million bucks to fight him again (which is news to everybody). "Why, George?" "Because he's either scared or crazy."

Of course, Ali is neither, but is just trying to get in a few more paydays before facing the big three, Foreman, Frazier and Norton, one of whom will get him. (My guess from his table talk is that he wants to fight Norton last, if ever.) As champions go, Ali has been more honorable than most in not ducking contenders. Patterson and Frazier fought nameless stiffs from the outback, and Foreman went a year without fighting at all. Still, George is patiently feeding his private obsession, like some giant animal he keeps on a leash. He says that his water was definitely poisoned in

Zaire; that fighting on the ropes isn't fighting at all; that he won't fight no one else except Ali; that he is the greatest. On and on he mumbles. For me, I'd as soon hear a coyote howling outside my tent.

The Lyle fight is a virtually empty pallet for Ali's temperament to work with. There is a persistent rumor that Ali is doing it to keep Lyle out of jail for allegedly taking a pot shot at a car containing his wife. Dundee denies it, but it feeds the myth that there is always something bigger than boxing about Ali. And the fact remains that Ali did sign for the match shortly after the arrest, and that Lyle treats him with the greatest deference before, during and after the fight.

With no opponent to worry about, Ali goes to the usual extremes to amuse himself, and to devise new jokes within the limited grammar of boxing. The day before the fight he maddens the promoters by sparring, which can lead to stubbed toes, pulled groins and postponements. Not only that, but he is fighting four rounds without intermission. Another Ali first. The partners race in and out frantically replacing each other at his midriff. For most of the time, he waxes fetal, but then for what seems like two minutes, he lets himself get hit directly in the stomach *while he talks*—a great test for public speakers.

Afterwards he breaks out his new line in advertising, the "rope-a-dope" style (he enunciates it slowly for reporters, no doubt the way he memorized it himself), which will be supplemented this time by the "mirage": i.e., phantom appearances in the middle of the ring, with Ali's face materializing like the Flying Dutchman, luring his opponent back into the ropes. A sermon often repeated causes the mind to wander,

and I remember how Ali used to say that the object of boxing was not to get hit; yet now the object seems to be to get hit as much as possible. Is there no middle position?

In *Sting Like a Bee,* Jose Torres says that Ali's rope fighting is neither tactical nor energy-saving, but simply a habit he picked up during his layoff. In that same period, *Esquire* ran a cover picture of Ali tied to a stake and riddled with arrows, which seems to be the religious equivalent of his new style.

The weigh-in the next day is the quietest in years. In Lewis Carroll's words, "There was silence supreme, not a shriek, not a scream." Well, not exactly. There are

Travelling with brother Rachaman.

a few shrieks. But Ali is still following his policy of non-aggression toward Lyle, which grows to epidemic proportions during the fight itself.

He dedicates the fight to his latest cause, the defense of Hurricane Carter and gives a high-minded press conference on the subject (it is not true that he calls a press conference every time he goes to the john). Since fights are rarely dedicated to anyone, this is yet another ingenious device for making his every move a landmark. Hurricane, you will recall, was a ferocious middleweight, later jailed on a murder rap which seems now to be coming unstuck. Ali speaks briefly. He is impressed that the committee is headed by prominent white men, some of whom "own shopping centers in the New Jersey area." He hasn't mastered the facts of the case, and needs to be prompted, but he does come up with a thrilling Western parable about someone riding a hundred miles lickety-split to find the only witness, who in turn rides up just as the noose tightens around the suspect's neck.

You will get few better illustrations of Ali's mind at work. He probably never will get those facts straight, but he'll improve the story until it is ready for film.

He is further impressed that Carter has refused to watch TV in the slam—no guilty man would have done that, he says. Only an innocent man would dispense with his telly. ("That's right," says Rachaman.) This must surely be a unique defense. He also describes the case as a New Jersey Watergate, leaving one to wonder what he thinks *that* was about, and adds that he once spent four days in jail himself on a traffic violation, and near went crazy. So he dedicates this fight to Carter.

If Carter wants it. For it turns out to be the veriest dog—and I'd draw a shroud over it except that it shows how Ali the boxer still has the power to make an ass out of Ali the celebrity and vice versa.

He tries more consciously to entertain than he used to, but his new style is so ugly that it's like someone imitating a hunchback for laughs. Against Wepner, his new style was mildly amusing, because Wepner is a clown in his own right and came flobbering after Ali like a circus seal. But against a fighter who simply stands still and watches, it becomes ridiculous. Ali crouching by himself on the ropes with no one to talk to isn't funny, but slightly pathetic.

Thus by sheer inertia, Lyle strikes a crippling blow at Ali the entertainer. Even the "mirage" doesn't work tonight. Ali materializes all right and sticks out his face to be hit, but Lyle simply looks at it, flaps a paw, stands there. For the first time since the Oscar Bonavena fight in 1971, Ali is booed for dullness. "Hit him in the tongue," says a man, just like the old days.

This is ominous in terms of multi-million dollar promotions. Because there will surely be more and more Lyles waiting for him and angrier boos, now that the secret is out. Nobody is going to fight him the old way anymore, beating on his iron stomach. Which is bad news for the entertainer and the boxer both.

Because while Ali is writhing foolishly against the ropes, Lyle is piling up a modest lead on points for at least doing something, like standing up straight. In the end it will take a knockout for Ali to win, a safe bet against Lyle, but what about Joe Bugner, his next opponent, young, dull and iron-jawed? And what about Norton, prancing around the lobby tonight like Tarzan, and

Foreman brooding darkly a few feet away from me, and the whole murderers' row that's waiting out in the alley for him?

I sense the shadows of eventual defeat tonight as Ali wheels overhead, obliged to dance intermittently, with his stomach sighing slightly as he changes gears, like a tired businessman on the dance floor. At one point he even has to stick Lyle with a panicky right to make his own getaway. He is not directing the comedy tonight, but wearing the baggy pants himself.

He gets his knockout in the 11th round, and for 58 seconds he looks as good as he ever has. One straight right in particular could be shipped straight to the Hall of Fame; and he calls on his servant the ref to stop the fight, none too soon. But he has thrown a scare into his corner. "He's losing the championship," Rachaman announces grimly in the 10th. This is going too far in the way of cheap thrills. Bundini, who has been relatively subdued, bursts into tears. Pacheco warns that a cut around Ali's eye could turn into something—a new problem for the champ, whose skin is so perfect Pacheco tells me you could make ladies' purses out of it. There is a sense of things unraveling.

The post-fight stampede, which usually resembles a crowd scene from *Intolerance*, is no more than a resigned trickle. Around the nation people snap off their dials testily if they have any sense. The fight was on national TV, "so the underprivileged can see me," but even the underprivileged shouldn't be subjected to this. He has had a bad night, both as fighter and entertainer, the kind of night that people throw eggs at.

Why? Well, Ali the boxer says that his new tactics save his strength and exhaust the other fellow. But Ali the entertainer must know that nobody pays 100 bucks to watch a man save his strength, or drives through downtown traffic to see the other one get exhausted. Does he think the mere sight of himself is worth all that gold?

His critics, still reeling from Zaire, get a new lease on life and they come bouncing back with a fresh cliché. Joe Louis wouldn't have done it. When the sainted Joe formed his Bum-of-the-Month Club back in 1941, they say, he at least fought his bums, he didn't crouch in a corner and make faces at them. So public enemy Ali is suddenly up on a new charge—that of impersonating a heavyweight.

To root for Ali is to share his artfully concocted ups and downs. Thus, as the critics rally, the true-believers are forced into their own rope-a-dopes. After the smugness of Zaire, they hadn't expected to have to defend their boy again so soon. Yet here he is displaying himself to the underprivileged for a one and a half million guarantee—and dogging it. And now he's talking about Malaysia and Cairo and wherever the money tree grows and the suckers bloom. Is this what the draft board fight was about, and the bloody comeback and the championship of the Universe? Just another all-American hustle? Ali has found a brand new way to madden people: short-changing them.

I ask Angelo Dundee about this after the fight and he seems to be in real distress, if only as a connoisseur. Does anybody actually enjoy watching this new style, the Masochist One-Step? "They like the style because Ali does it," says Angelo. "With anyone else, they'd abhor it." Which can only mean that, consciously or otherwise, Ali is exploiting his celebrity to get away with murder. "I don't know how long he can take this garbage," concludes Angelo.

At the next day's press conference, I decide to put it to Ali himself. "If you were a fan would you like to watch this new style?" He pauses, appears to think. "Not for more than four or five rounds," he says, and that's the best I can get. The day before, someone asked him why he was predicting eight rounds for Lyle, and he said "for the sake of TV." Lash the two answers together and you get the real one. Ali respects TV scheduling as one of life's verities, and if he's listed for half an hour, he'll give you half an hour, of whatever quality. This is how he saves the sport and debases it simultaneously. Before his reign too many fights were ending in the first one or two rounds, which is nature's way when trucks collide, but was killing it for TV, which is the gateway to the mass mind.

There is no doubt from his early fights or from tonight's last round that he can put away mediocrities as fast as he wants to. But he's in the habit of dawdling these days and giving you a few more rounds of profile ("suppose I try to knock them out and get tired" is his excuse) and this has plunged him into his seventh crisis or whatever. Because until recently he could string things out entertainingly by dancing, but now he is like a garrulous storyteller, or journalist, holding the floor for the sake of holding the floor. You still get to see lots of Ali, but in a manner that only Andy Warhol (director of *Sleeping,* a nine hour saga) could love.

This at least is the semi-out-of-shape Ali of the moment, who is hungrily raking in his "fool's gold" as he calls it, and cashing every chip of his Zaire glory. When he is trying, as in tonight's last round, he is as

good as ever; but he no longer looks good when he isn't trying, except against sparring partners and assorted stiffs, who aren't trying to kill him. These he can spar with in tank towns and tank countries as long as his name holds up. But against even semi-respectable professionals, he can only be funny in the gaps, i.e., at the beginning of each round when he can stalk out double-time like Jacques Tati and meet in the other guy's corner; or between rounds, or during clinch-breaks, or the day before.

Why he wants the money so much we'll never know for sure. When Snyder asked him if it was good for the nation's youth to have such a greedy man for a hero, he rambled about how everybody earns as much as he can, but this is not a fit answer for either an artist or saint. Leaving aside the inscrutable imperatives of Muslim finance, we are left with a man who craves money like Scrooge and gives it away like foreign aid. Part of this is just a professional mannerism. Fraser Scott, the writing boxer, says he never met a stingy boxer, even among the pigs: buying drinks is part of the endless battle to get the crowd on your side. It shows power and it buys power. But with Ali it goes further. It also secures him a small kingdom of dependents, whom he can care for, protect and dominate: starting with the Royal Family itself.

Which brings me back to my own Mc-Guffin, which hears a different drum and walks between the cracks.

It is apparent by now that brother Rachaman is in a hyper-excited condition this week, and it carries right into the fight. I don't know much about Rachaman except that he seems troubled. As a boy, he is said to have been both bright and angelic (young Cassius was the family devil) but now he

222

seems morose and purposeless. For a while he was a fighter himself, but he wasn't quite good enough. On the night of the first Ali-Frazier fight, he was knocked out earlier in the proceedings, putting a slight extra strain on his brother. Maybe Muhammad asked him to quit after that, or maybe his own good sense suggested it. Anyway, since then he has had no discernible occupation except travelling with Ali and identifying with him totally. (Actually, they're both named Ali, but for clarity's sake, the name still refers to Muhammad.)

Tonight he is in quite an uproar, expressing the concern that *Ali* might reasonably have felt over being behind on points. And afterwards, he does the ranting from ringside that Ali used to do for himself. It is as if Rachaman is taking over some of the secondary aspects of the persona—mainly the angry ones.

As with the other Clay males, it is hard to tell if he is really angry until you get up close. From 100 feet away, he seems to be picking a fight with someone in the middle distance, or demanding that a cus-

tomer be thrown out, or declaring war; but when I get closer, I realize he isn't shouting at anyone in particular. "He is the greatest," or words to that effect, seems to be the message.

Rachaman continues to simmer all evening and later tries to keep me out of the dressing room for no apparent reason except that I'm white. It is in marked contrast with Muhammad's serenity over the last few days, as if the family rage has all been siphoned into Rachaman, the former angel.

Well, not quite all of it. Cassius Clay, Sr. turns up at the press conference with his own case of the mean reds. Ali introduces him politely as "my father Cassius Clay, Senior," pronouncing the prickly name with respect, but the old man is in no mood for pleasantries. "I made him," he shouts, "he ain't learned nothing since he was 12." Ali smiles indulgently. "You mean I was just as good when I was aged 12 as I am now?" "Better," shouts Cassius, Sr.

He says a lot more than that, but it's hard to follow. He talks fast when he's excited, and the words get garbled, like misspellings. His feeling for language is intuitive like his son's and not analytic, and it is easy to see how Ali acquired verbal brilliance in that company without achieving literacy. "Now you see why I talk the way I do," says Ali, smiling at his father.

It is a touching scene. Mr. Clay is proud of his son or he wouldn't be on the caravan. But he also wants a piece of the credit, and a few moments of your attention. Considering the amount of limelight that there is around here, this seems reasonable. At any rate, Ali seems to understand it perfectly, and he treats Cassius, Sr.

Mr. and Mrs. Cassius Clay, Sr. in Zaire.

with much sweetness and patience. Maybe they were buddies on the good days hopping trolleys and showing off, while Mr. Clay watched the girls. And if there were bad days, the score is more than settled now, as Mr. Clay follows his son from town to town trying to catch a thimbleful of glory.

I am struck especially by the unruffled way in which Ali responds. Usually a childhood fear leaves some small trace on the nerves: one's voice rises and quickens, or becomes deliberately calm. But Ali is incorrigibly relaxed. If there ever was fear, he has conquered it exultantly, root and branch. Maybe preparing your mind to fight Liston and Foreman does that for you.

If there ever was fear. Another possibility occurs to me later in the dressing room, and I mention it for what it's worth. Rachaman at this point is still carrying on about nothing in particular, and finally Ali goes over and says something to him. Obviously something calming, because Rachaman subsides immediately.

And I think that's just the way his mama would have done it. In fact, Ali handles the two fractious males in the family just like a mother. They are both gifted but they haven't quite made it in a world where fame is everything, and he understands that. The only fame they can have is his, and he shares it gladly. But he can't give it away. The world wants him and not them. Celebrity-worship is viciously exclusive. So they follow him round, catching the reflections, both unable just to give up and go home.

Cassius, Sr. does of course go home between fights to live a pretty exuberant life of his own. But he is drawn to the circus atmosphere of boxing; it is a place where a fellow like himself can operate. Yet when he gets there, there's his son at the center of the ring every single time: it makes a man peeved, that's all.

With Rachaman, the relationship seems deeper. One feels that Ali may possibly have become a Muslim to please Rachaman, and he may stay one to please him

too: at any rate, he is more of one when Rachaman is around. He loves to oblige people in general, but with Rachaman there seems to be a special protective quality, which apparently goes back to when they were children. Ali seems to have felt it his duty from the start to protect his little brother, against God knows what: street gangs, night terrors, whatever fears were going round.

So this is the thought that struck me, for better or worse. Is it possible that little Cassius was not afraid for himself but for his brother or somebody else? That the blows he fends off are aimed at Rachaman? And that the two of them fled their past together like orphans of the storm, and changed names together to begin a new life with Elijah? Anyway Rachaman's hatred of the white man seems more on his brother's behalf than his own. It is Ali's dressing room that he protects. Ali's speeches that he defends against invisible hecklers. The white world may pretend it likes Ali right now, but you can't fool Rachaman.

Whatever the exact geometry, family love is central to Ali. From such trivia as his shyness with strangers and his inability to dance, one guesses that he didn't have much else for years. In fact it was so much a part of him that he had to tear himself violently from it to be anybody at all. But having done so, he now reigns over it benignly, protecting each member according to his own kind.

Las Vegas is my last stop. The celestial omnibus is heading East, into real Muslim country where Ali can polish his theology and engage in a 15-round love-feast with Joe Bugner (aargh). But one has to get off someplace, and Vegas, where the money flows like wine and your only home is a hotel room, seems as good a bus stop as any.

So I say goodbye to my new friends. I tell Pacheco I am presenting him as an unscrupulous con man, and he responds with his dirtiest laugh. There ensues a solemn exchange of cigars with Dundee, and I tell him to let me know the next time he has a fighter as interesting as Ali. His answer is the saddest and most certain prophecy ever made: Never. From Luis Sarria, I get a nod and a wink, which is like an interminable after-dinner speech from anyone else. Don King says, "Make me big. Just make me big." OK, Don, you're big. And so the bus pulls out of the desert jingling with silver—another good week in Vegas for Ali and the 40 thieves.

And the path of Ali continues to follow the sun, opening up new territories as American traders have always done; and Ali the great black American plants his flag where white Americans fear more and more to tread. Never mind that when he gets to Malaysia he praises the air-conditioning. American salesmen have always talked smaller than their real achievements. And Ali knows at least as much about Malaysia as Standard Oil or even Dean Rusk.

The road to Malaysia proves to be as comic as anything in a Hope & Crosby movie, as the clown and the minister continue to horn in uproariously on each other's acts. The clown announces the Malaysian Waltz (instructions to follow, when he thinks of some), while the minister intones his absolute, 99%-positive resignation from boxing, inspired by a local spiritual adviser, who has been helping him get his head together for the last few days. (Significantly, his latest daddy is a Sunni, or orthodox, Moslem—of a group that had no truck with Elijah.)

At this point, Ali the banker chimes in and says he doesn't need the money anyway. He rattles his pockets: two million in cash and two more in investments. It beats brain damage. For good measure, Ali the film star adds that he is about to star in the movie of his own life, "The Greatest," and has no time for fighting. The stage is filling with Alis, entering like ghosts.

The model husband and father bat clean-up. He wants more time with his wife (who cried when he left the U.S.) and children. It is heartbreaking to have to leave them so often. By now, there can hardly be a dry eye in the press box. At least it is too much for Dick Young, who writes the story we have all known for months: that there is a constant stream of foxes in his room, assuaging his loneliness, including one Veronica Porche, whom Belinda is said to call his other wife. I have seen Miss Porche actually baby-sitting with Muhammad's children while the master slept in the next room, and am willing to accept her as a nursemaid or whatever he prefers.

But there is a limit to the number of ways Muhammad can have it. The winking cop-out is that the girls won't leave him alone, but to the naked eye the arrangement looks reciprocal. ("Watch the vibrating bus," said a waggish hanger-on in Miami.) If Ali is really giving up boxing on account of Belinda, it could be that the high-stepping side of the boxing life is too much for him after all.

Likewise, the minister threatens to split his pants on the retirement issue. Rumor has it that the Bugner fight is wheezing at the box office, and there's nothing like a little retirement talk to pep it up. Big Don King almost burst into tears when he first heard Ali's threat to quit, and offered "to crawl on my belly like a reptile" to avert it; but the next day, he announces that he's "too proud to beg," which suggests that some private reassurance has gotten him up off his belly. And sure enough, the next Frazier fight is arranged in a twinkling for some eight million smackers, which can buy an awful lot of spiritual advice.

In short, Ali is on the brink of being a real laughingstock, out of control of the joke, if his various souls insist on fighting like cats in a sack. His new opponent, public interest, is not quite the sap he takes it for, and this indiscriminate whoring after headlines, any headlines, makes a man first silly, then pathetic. People cross the street to avoid celebrities in this piteous condition.

But what kind of Ali do we want right now? He wishes you'd tell him. He was the perfect hero for an age of self-pity: a man who would protect us all, as he protects his family, if we only asked him to, and who protected *himself* by being passive. When his title was taken away, he just lay down like a student or a Buddhist monk and took it. And by so doing, he put the adult establishment to shame.

That was the heyday of the Christ-figure, and Ali was a dilly, even down to his parables. Dignified non-resistance came as easy to him as breathing. Long before he became a Muslim he never protested what was left of Jim Crow, but simply walked out where he wasn't wanted. He even taunted Bundini to tears once for making a scene in such a situation. Turning the other cheek is a rare virtue in a fighter, but it was the only way he could have won the flower-children. Thus, in final parody of the Gospels, the blood-soaked leader of a bloody profession wound up with an army of non-violent disciples.

But the times are, as he says, changing, and the butterfly had better change with them. The publicity creature senses this right away. Christ-figures are out and Superfly is in. So the rope-a-dope suddenly becomes an offensive weapon. He rechristens it "the Russian Tank" (detente has not gone unnoticed) and uses it to charge his opponents like a maddened embryo: no longer self-pity but a parody of self-pity.

We loved him as a martyr, but at current prices he's no martyr now. He turns off questions about his draft evasion with vague remarks about "doing what's right" that might apply to brushing his teeth, and he has not been a zealous supporter of amnesty. That was yesterday's hornet's-nest. Today the talk is about his accomplishments. He has done martyrdom; now, like his young followers, he is doing success.

And this has won him his strangest fan club of all. The squares love him now. He has become, by magic, their kind of nigger: self-reliant, keeps to his own kind, harm-lessly entertaining. He also feeds their sense of black mystery, giving off emanations of a zestier world that delights them in small doses. In this sense his separatism has reproduced a Southern type of situation. We can truly love Negroes on those terms, and feel that a little contact with them enriches our own lives. The small-town businessmen who crowd around him so joyously are absolved of bigotry—"You see, I like Ali! He's so clean."

Thus the mantle of Joe Louis awaits him after all. And in his new Chamber of Commerce state of mind it seems to suit him. He can go on being a devil, because that's part of his charm—in fact, his naughtiness seems almost old-fashioned by now and ready for the nostalgia bank.

But squares get older and their love is fleeting. If Ali wants to hang on to the youth market, which makes and destroys celebrities, he will soon need something more than his current imitation of a mischievous Rotarian. In a period of exhaustion, it's fine. But who knows what the tots will be brewing up in a year or two?

Ali will undoubtedly think of something. Meanwhile he has his preaching. Unfortunately, Muslim doctrine, since Elijah's death, has become rather pale and may not be enough to feed the fire in his belly or the expectations in his audience. Already Wallace has declared the movement open to whites (there has so far been no great rush) and it has lost its defining racist trademark. He has also opened its books (revealing 42 million in assets), so there goes its secrecy. And Wallace, a rather neutral character, seems unlikely to brew up any more of Elijah's spectacular theology that so enthralled young Cassius. (Elijah's wonder stories were originally designed to wow blacks fresh off the farm and don't seem right for young businessmen on the way up.)

So all the reasons he had for joining so ardently have been shot down, one by one, leaving him with a real estate conglomerate and a vague allegiance to World

Islam. Some of the other members who joined for racial identity will want to hang on to that for grim life, and they will try to use Ali as they appeared to use him in Cleveland. And a resurgence of race warfare, brought on by hard times, might find him listening. But right now there is just not enough box office in racism. The 25,000 crowd hollering for him at the Kuala Lumpur airport are a powerful persuader simply to go international and broaden his temple. And World Islam not only multiplies his ratings but, in a pinch, his wives. If the obliging Wallace were to go along with some *de facto* polygamy too, it would be a sizable step in Ali's moccasins. After all, seldom has a religion been so willing to tailor itself to its star.

Will he be a religious leader himself? I asked an insider, who said, "Are you kidding? He can't even lead himself. He *follows* himself." More specifically, my source added that Ali lacks the guile and diplomacy for religious leadership, and would be hopeless at the in-fighting on which religion thrives.

That would seem to be that for now. The Muslims were always threatening to fall apart even under the shrewd Elijah, so without him there could be a death struggle for identity. And Ali's talents for generalship have so far been totally absorbed by boxing. But he is only 33 and growing; and if he finds his face slipping out the back end of *People* magazine, he might find a religious title irresistible.

Could he be a real king outside of a story? As usual, half of him probably could and half of him couldn't. At one moment, he will tell you how he makes all his own decisions, and at the next he will say it isn't up to him who he fights next. Both statements are as true as he wants them to be, as he careens between active and passive, willfulness and total dependence. In the ring, he is God: Pacheco says the only cornerman he needs is a mirror; but outside he is now father, now son, now free spirit. If the three-part Christian God somehow

images the human psyche, Ali is a classic rendering.

If he doesn't get his stuff together soon, he would be a high-risk leader. Worse, he would be bored. But celebrities are expected to do *something*, and Ali does have at least one peculiar advantage to the Muslims: his fame and charm serve to unify this frenzied group and give it personality. Even the puritan wing, which deplored Elijah's habit of snuggling with his secretaries, seems merely bemused by Ali's leering cupidity.

If he were to become a leader, in fact or by example, where would he lead? One problem with victim-figures is that they can turn nasty when on top. Ali's admirers are distressed and puzzled when he occasionally delays a kill in order to humiliate a well-beaten opponent, yet this is only the other side of masochist behavior. Don't ever let a masochist get the upper hand; his vengeance has been feeding a long time.

Fortunately, Ali seems to be growing more merciful—as a fighter at least—as if he had worked that particular poison out of his system. If he still humiliates Dundee by commanding him to fetch and carry, it is all in fun, an acting-out of a spent sadism. In Cleveland, where things got tense around him, he reverted to cruelty. But he had the wisdom to return to Miami from there and calm down. He *wants* to be nice.

So much the case for mellowing. On the other side lie the incalculable effects of aging. His virtues are such youthful ones, and they could wrinkle badly. When he no longer feels a funky joy at being alive, what will he feel instead? Relief that he's proved his point, or bitterness that it's all over?

Probably both, and a lot besides. Quitting boxing has to be a sickening wrench. For twenty years, time has stood still while he boxed. Now he must pick it up again where he left it at 13.

Will it be too late to retrain the lush brain cells that nature gave him, for peaceful purposes? Studies show that children who don't learn to read and write go on developing their instinctive intelligence

231

long after the literates have quit. And Ali's intelligence is of this sort, a genuine animal wisdom like Marlon Brando's, that makes him perversely attractive to the inarticulate generation. For all his gabble, he is one of them.

Something tells me he won't settle for this. He has enormous respect for trained intelligence, and would like to add this to his repertoire. He would love to be a sage and will work on that. A lot depends now on who gets his ear. Malcolm X is long gone, and Bundini's wisdom isn't getting any younger, but Herbert and Wallace Muhammad seem at least shrewd and level-headed, and I see them sheltering him against the charms of fanaticism as long as they can. When he discovers how difficult real intelligence is, he may get sore all over again.

But reading this man's future beyond next week is a fool's errand. Right now he is improving visibly as a platform performer, sharpening his timing, as he does in the ring, by endless repetition. At a recent booksellers' convention he charmed the socks off the denizens with lines he'd used a hundred times before. His ad libs are now so sharp that you can't tell the real ones from the retreads. His sparkle, in boxing and in life, comes from plodding dedication.

This may be the most interesting of all his contradictions. For an apparently flighty man, he is willing to endure bone-crushing boredom to produce just the right effect of carelessness. Like Fred Astaire, he labors long hours over his jauntiness. Which is not to say that his high spirits are faked, but only that they are harnessed to an iron discipline. The ebullient kid from Louisville has become a polished global entertainer by sheer hard work.

That is why his interviews and press conferences have such a curious air of irrelevance. They are simply rehearsals, and he uses them to run through his new material regardless of the questions. Like most comics, he needs fresh audiences constantly;

and if the sports-writers sound jaded, remember, they have been sitting in the studio a long time.

Would his stuff seem funny if it wasn't Muhammad Ali's? Or would it wilt like the rope-a-dope? At the moment it doesn't matter because his meteor is up there and blazing. And as long as he can dredge more great fights out of his magnificent body and its seven crazy owners, his jokes will be the funniest you ever heard.

But what happens to the meteor when he loses? Even he doesn't know, which is why he keeps fighting, driving his body and spirit to the limit, and using every trick of self-preservation in his magic kit. He may still be recognized on every street ten years from now, but he can't be sure—Frankie Avalon, Fabian, the stars of his youth, who'd know them now? Warhol's Age of the 15-Minute Celebrity is a stiff challenge. So he stages another fight, and another.

The race is on between body and spirit and boredom. Imagination has kept him going in a dogged profession, but imagination requires fresh food every day, and you can almost hear it growling louder and louder. Is there a new way to train he hasn't thought of? Why not hold the next fight in an igloo? Who's the greatest thumb-wrestler? Some night a hungry fighter with nothing else on his mind will interrupt his thoughts and scatter them. Which would give him a chance for that last great comeback, and it would be at last as super-colossal as the *Third* Coming of course. But boxing stories wind down eventually and one thinks of the last days of Sugar Ray and Joe Louis himself—coming back, not coming back. Who cares? Ali the celebrity would be much better off retiring if he can keep the fighter away from the bright lights.

Here his interest in Marciano and Tunney, both white and undefeated, may come in handy. His first clumsy flirtation with retirement may not be altogether a hoax but more like dipping your toe in boiling water and yanking it out again.

Until recently black athletes could not afford to retire (which has produced such prodigies of longevity as Satchel Paige and Archie Moore), and Ali has kept the habit. He is not a carefree man. But he can afford it now. Whatever anxieties he may have picked up around his father's house have been beaten senseless by payday after payday, and he is ready to enter the world of pure celebrity, where he doesn't need pantomime build-ups with Wepners and Foremans and other terrestrial characters, but can be himself. Alone. At last.

The only trouble now is the public, and divining what it wants. Ali became a hero by defying the government and sticking to his guns about it; yet when he talks about the beliefs that made him do it, we yawn, like the kids in Cleveland: "Do the shuffle, Ali. Make us laugh." We want our celebrities to stay the same forever, until they bore us—and then to come back on appointed feast-days and bore us again. (These are known as TV specials.) The death of God has left us in a fine mess celebrity-wise, but photography came along in time to give us new ones on the theory that if you show anybody's image often enough, even Walter Cronkite's, that person becomes a god by accumulation. The more you see the picture, the more likely you are to see the man; and once you see the man, you have to see more pictures—until bedrooms hang like shrines. Even Jesus Christ could only come back as a superstar.

Ali is now the king of these picture-gods, and as such he must be touched, verified, asked to identify himself: "Dance. Say something about Howard Cosell. Do something we *recognize*." People follow him with shining eyes, just to make sure he exists. "My God, it's Ali!"—such is our prayer.

But how can he ensure that his picture will go on being taken and circulated forever and ever, and not just on feast-days? Frantically, as he leaves boxing, he tries to diversify, and we get this flush of crazy headlines. We've gladly bought him as a model husband and father, but he also wants to be able to say to the students at Harvard, "I judge a school by how many sisters are around." Likewise we've bought him as an entertainer, but he calls that stuff "foolishness": we are to understand that he is also a preacher, a serious man. He tells the students, "I had to tell you that there are more sides in Muhammad Ali than you see on TV."

But we can't cope with all these personalities. We want the one he started with, *the funny one.* So, reluctantly, he interrupts his ministry to give us another burst of that. The response he gets from just being funny is so full-blooded, and the response to his preaching so numb and flat, that he falls back on clowning like an addict even at his most serious moments. The great man of Zaire and the laughing boy of Louisville still play the boards together, inextricably entwined.

The graduation day session at Harvard is a fine illustration of how he fights for his many faces against a public that only wants one. After giving his lecture, as warned, about the heart and its intoxications, he tells the graduates that "people don't pay for that, they pay for foolishness." But so, it turns out later, do graduates.

"Remember who you are today, because when you make it you have a tendency to forget what you were yesterday." Ali is poised classically between the motions of humility, which is his new game, and a real and rueful self-knowledge—except that with him the two are one: the act is real. "I'm from Louisville, Kentucky, a little black boy who made $18 a week (how?) and wanted to be Golden Gloves champion."

The sense of loss is genuine—he can conjure up a golden youth that is as real as a good poem—but at the same time he knows that a sense of loss is a terrific thing to have in itself, a kingly emotion. Did Keats really care that much about nightingales? He did for one night, and that's all that counts.

This rendition of *My Old Kentucky Home* should have been enough for the grads: proof that his serious act is now ready to play after years of private polish in living room and mosque.

Yet the story has it that what really brought the house down was the Ali shuffle and his imitation of Howard Cosell.

Back outside the glass and safe in my living room, I see once more the face on the tube, big brother or son or mortal enemy or whatever you want to see, and I wonder how this shy, brooding man does it. And I realize that, as with all great actors, what you see on the screen is real, and all the rest is tinsel. In the ring and in the headlines, he acts out his whole range of emotions—love, hate, fear, vengeance. If he sometimes does this in private (and he doesn't often), it is only because he has shrunk the stage. It is still theater. His real emotions are locked so deep within him that even he doesn't recognize them. He can only find them by acting, talking, dancing. Between shows, the man behind the screen is as neutral as a psychic medium. When he isn't performing, he is not so much dull as non-existent. There is an awesome blankness about him. His obsession with women is not just a need to be champion in one more field, but a function of emptiness and boredom. In repose, life ceases: he is nobody. I asked him if he ever liked other sports, and he said quite desolately, no, he never had.

But fortunately, he is seldom, if ever, in repose. His imagination can always cook up something to amuse the bored child in him. Already he has sprouted a terrific new past for himself among the working poor—although such boys rarely have the time or expenses for 108 amateur fights—and he has become once again the baddest bicycle thief in Louisville (but only after they'd stolen his, mind you). It seems he also threw his handy Olympic gold medal into the Ohio River after a racial affront in a restaurant. But since we know that he was still

239

wearing his U.S.A. trunks for some time later, it's possible he hadn't severed all ties with his country.

I don't doubt the truth of these or other, equal and opposite legends. The point is that the real story of Ali is the story of his imagination, and not what Bundini contemptuously calls the facts, which are simply his raw materials. All we ask of Ali is top quality entertainment and myths we can use, and these he continues to provide in uneven abundance. For instance, he is considering a trip to Red China, and already we can see him in the land of Confucius and the Red Guard, swapping small talk with Chairman Mao and asking about the foxes and the agriculture, and leavening it all with a wisecrack for the folks on TV: "Chairman Mao called me a nigger. I ain't got nothing against them Tibetans."

Whatever you think of the man you've been looking at, the world would have been an immeasurably duller place without him. And he's determined to keep things the way they are, even if it means giving up being serious altogether—at least the celebrity-creature is, and that's all we've seen so far. Someday Muslim wisdom, or even his own, may drag him from the limelight, but it won't be easy. He worshipped at the shrine of fame a long time before he heard of Allah, and he still bows in that direction every time he sees a Brownie or a typewriter. So the kind of Ali we get is still up to us, a reflection of what he thinks he sees on our faces. Right now, we seem to want a laughing hero, and we've got one. But if the times should call for something a little more sinister, there's always a hint he could provide that too. Whether it's a put-on or not, it is this tension that keeps every eye on Ali. And without those eyes he would be alone.

So he doubles every effort: smiling, snarling, signing autographs, even confessing selected sins—anything it takes to keep the world watching; to keep his place safe in the sun and out of the dark.

240

Charlie Powell fight, 1963.

Acknowledgements

The first and third sections of this book are based largely on secondary sources, which include mountains of press clippings, rugged hours spent in bar-room think tanks, and finally my own head, which recreated Ali stone by stone in its own image, as writers must. A rough bibliography for Ali-philes would have to contain at least the following: virtually the whole of *Sports Illustrated,* which has covered Ali about as thoroughly as a subject can be covered, and in particular everything by Mark Kram, the resident Ali genius, along with Gilbert Rogin, Martin Kane and Tex Maule; ditto *Ebony Magazine,* for its three dimensional pieces (I think especially of Hans J. Massaquoi's of April 1969) which seem to get closer than the white magazines ever do; and finally a host of individual writers, listed in no particular order. Jack Olsen's *Black is Best, the Riddle of Cassius Clay* provides invaluable material on the Louisville background, to which Jose Torres and John Cottrell add useful touches and much besides in their books *Sting Like a Bee* and *Muhammad Ali who once was Cassius Clay.* Robert Lipsyte (in the New York Times Magazine *passim*) is superb on the exile years, particularly the Buck White episode. The estimable George Plimpton captures Zaire in print and conversation as only an old Africa hand can, and Norman Mailer as only a Norman Mailer can (Norman's influence is so pervasive and voodoo-like that I decided not to finish his pieces in *Playboy).* C. Erik Lincoln's book *The Black Muslims in America* is still the best word on that subject, but for ongoing news from this volatile organization I have relied largely on the Amsterdam News and William Brashler's fine article in *New York Magazine.* Jack Richardson wrote a fine color piece called *Ali on Peachtree* for *Harpers* (Jan. '71) on Ali's return to the ring against Quarry in Atlanta and the anonymous toilers at Time and Newsweek filled in cracks all along the line.

On a personal level, I would like to thank especially my old good friends Larry Merchant, Vic Ziegel and Joe Flaherty for sharing the hard-earned insights that less generous writers would save for themselves; Dick Young for uncommon courtesy around the fight scene; Jimmy Jacobs for running hours of film at a moment's notice, and passing on his unrivalled knowledge; Joe Okpaku the Nigerian writer for helpful advice on the black scene here and in Africa; and variously John Condon, Red Smith, Pete Hamill, Hal Conrad and a host of others for making this the pleasantest beat I ever covered. Angelo Dundee and Ferdie Pacheco get theirs in the text: I trust we will meet again soon.

Finally, thanks to my friend and partner Neil Leifer, with whom I worked, played, talked and drank so closely that by now I consider this book his as much as mine; to my editor Jay Acton for leg and phone work beyond the call of duty and for his valuable insights at Hollywood Park race track, to designer Will Hopkins, merely the best, and to our ring-master, the ineffable Lawrence Schiller for getting all of us and the idea together in the first place and driving it like a Roman Gladiator to completion.

Photo Credits

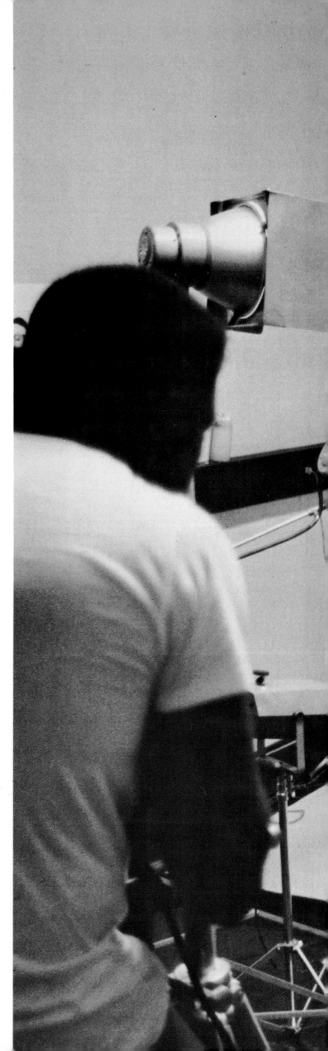

Posing for Lowell Riley,
Herbert Muhammad's photographer.

Special effect photography by Phillip Leonian.

The editors are deeply indebted to the late Frank Agolia, picture-editor of *Sports Illustrated*, whose deft eye culled a major share of the pictures in this book from the magazine's voluminous files. Frank's tireless dedication and warmhearted enthusiasm will be missed by the photographic community.

Professional Record

1.
Tunney Hunsaker
Louisville
Oct. 29, 1960
Decision in 6

2.
Herb Siler
Miami Beach
Dec. 27, 1960
KO in 4th

3.
Tony Esperti
Miami Beach
Jan. 17, 1961
KO in 3rd

4.
Jim Robinson
Miami Beach
Feb. 7, 1961
KO in 1st

5.
Donnie Fleeman
Miami Beach
Feb. 21, 1961
KO in 7th

Clay made his first professional prediction, claiming he would knock his man out in the third.

6.
Lamar Clark
Louisville
Apr. 19, 1961
KO in 2nd

Clay predicted that Clark, "would go in two."

7.
Duke Sabedong
Las Vegas
June 26, 1961
Decision in 10

8.
Alonzo Johnson
Louisville
July 22, 1961
Decision in 10

9.
Alex Miteff
Louisville
Oct. 7, 1961
KO in 6th

10.
Willie Besmanoff
Louisville
Nov. 29, 1961
KO in 7th

11.
Sonny Banks
New York
Feb. 11, 1962
KO in 4th

12.
Don Warner
Miami Beach
Feb. 28, 1962
KO in 4th

13.
George Logan
Los Angeles
Apr. 23, 1962
KO in 4th

Clay predicted, "Logan will go in 4."

14.
Billy Daniels
New York
May 19, 1962
KO in 7th

15.
Alejandro
Lavorante
Los Angeles
July 20, 1962
KO in 5th

"He will last five," was Clay's prediction. Lavorante died after his next fight.

16.
Archie Moore
Los Angeles
Nov. 15, 1962
KO in 4th

17.
Charlie Powell
Pittsburgh
Jan. 24, 1963
KO in 3rd

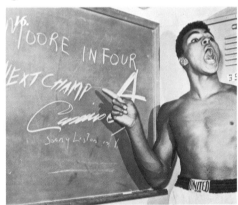

Clay's pre-fight statement was, "I'll retire that old man in 4. He's old enough to be my grand daddy." Three knockdowns in the 4th ended the fight.

18.
Doug Jones
New York
Mar. 13, 1963
Decision in 10

A newspaper strike in New York made Clay very unhappy. There was no publicity for his predicted 4th round KO. Just as well.

19.
Henry Cooper
London
June 18, 1963
KO in 5th

This was Clay's first professional fight outside the United States. He screamed to everyone that would listen that Cooper would fall in five rounds. In the fourth round Cooper landed a perfectly timed left hook that put Clay on the canvas for the second time in his professional career. Clay wobbled back to his corner, but when the bell rang for the fifth round he came out and won the fight as predicted.

20.
Sonny Liston
Miami Beach
Feb. 25, 1964
KO in 7th

An 8 to 1 underdog, a screaming Cassius Clay predicted that he would win the heavyweight championship in the eighth. But Liston didn't answer the bell for the seventh round. Clay stated afterwards that Liston didn't stay around for the extra round just to foil his prediction.

21.
Sonny Liston
Lewiston, Ma.
May 25, 1965
KO in 1st

A "Youth Center" gymnasium housed the second Liston fight. The fight was postponed six months because of Ali's hernia operation. After the one round knockout, Liston's license was suspended by the Boxing Commission, but he was cleared amid laughter.

22.
Floyd Patterson
Las Vegas
Nov. 22, 1965
KO in 12th

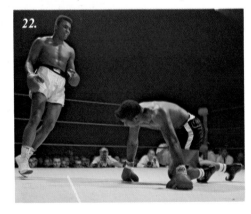

23.
George Chuvalo
Toronto, Canada
Mar. 29, 1966
Decision in 15

24.
Henry Cooper
London
May 21, 1966
KO in 6th

25.
Brian London
London
Aug. 6, 1966
KO in 3rd

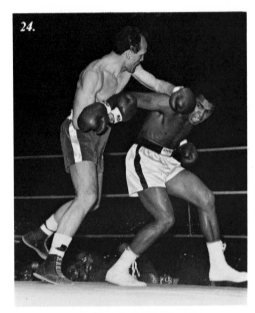

26.
Karl Mildenberger
Frankfurt
Sept. 10, 1966
KO in 12th

The first time a World Heavyweight Championship fight was ever held in Germany. The German "southpaw" Karl Mildenberger was stopped in the twelfth round.

27.
Cleveland
Williams
Houston
Nov. 14, 1966
KO in 3rd

28.
Ernie Terrell
Houston
Feb. 6, 1967
Decision in 15

The W.B.A., [World Boxing Association] had withdrawn recognition from Muhammad Ali two years earlier and had matched Eddie Machen against Ernie Terrell for their version of the heavyweight title. Terrell won, but nobody took the W.B.A. seriously. Finally, Ali took on Terrell to settle the issue anyway. Ali's unanimous decision regained him *full* recognition as heavyweight champion.

29.
Zora Folley
New York
Mar. 22, 1967
KO in 7th

Ali's last fight of the 1960s, before his title was taken away. He was considered to be at his brilliant best that night.

30.
Jerry Quarry
Atlanta
Oct. 26, 1970
KO in 3rd

31.
Oscar Bonavena
New York
Dec. 7, 1970
KO in 15th

Three and a half years later Ali was given a license to box in the state of Georgia. He took on the number one ranking contender Jerry Quarry after not fighting, seriously, since the Folley fight. (He had had a few exhibitions.) He stopped Quarry in three.

32.
Joe Frazier
New York
Mar. 8, 1971
Lost in 15th

For the first time in the history of boxing, two undefeated heavyweight champions fought for the title. Joe Frazier won a unanimous fifteen round decision to retain the World Heavyweight Championship, won in Ali's absence.

33.
Jimmy Ellis
Houston
July 26, 1971
KO in 12th

Four months after the Frazier fight Ali fought again against his former sparring partner, Jimmy Ellis. Ellis had won the W.B.A. heavyweight title during Ali's exile, and had lost it to Joe Frazier on Feb. 16, 1970. Ali stopped Ellis in twelve rounds, weighing 226, the heaviest of his pro career.

34.
Buster Mathis
Houston
Nov. 17, 1971
Decision in 12

35.
Jurgen Blin
Zurich
Dec. 26, 1971
KO in 7th

36.
Mac Foster
Tokyo
Apr. 1, 1972
Decision in 15

37.
George Chuvalo
Vancouver
May 1, 1972
Decision in 12

For the second time, Ali fails to knock out the Canadian punching bag.

38.
Jerry Quarry
Las Vegas
June 27, 1972
KO in 7th

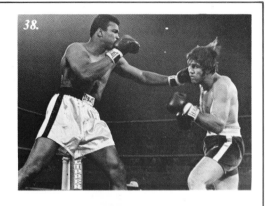

39.
Al Lewis
Dublin
July 19, 1972
KO in 11th

40.
Floyd Patterson
New York
Sept. 20, 1972
KO in 7th

41.
Bob Foster
Stateline
Nov. 21, 1972
KO in 8th

World light heavyweight champion, Bob Foster, cuts Ali for the first time but is knocked down seven times himself.

42.
Joe Bugner
Las Vegas
Feb. 14, 1973
Decision in 12

Joe Bugner is the British and European Champion.

43.
Ken Norton
San Diego
Mar. 31, 1973
Lost in 12th

This was supposed to be another "tune-up" for Ali, but he allegedly twisted his ankle while hitting a golf ball, didn't train and lost a split-decision. Ali had to take a back seat for a half year while his broken jaw healed.

44.
Ken Norton
Los Angeles
Sept. 10, 1973
Decision in 12

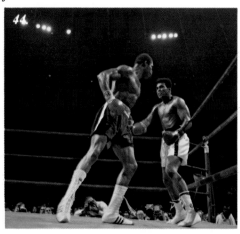

Ali trained for a tough re-match, and he got one. In the 12th and final round, Ali threw everything he had at the still vigorous Norton and just saved the fight on a split decision.

45.
Rudi Lubbers
Jakarta
Oct. 21, 1973
Decision in 12

A quick dollar. A "nothing" opponent.

46.
Joe Frazier
New York
Jan. 28, 1974
Decision in 12

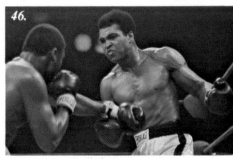

Frazier had lost the heavyweight title to George Foreman one year earlier, but Ali still wanted revenge. He had Frazier helpless in the second round, but referee Tony Perez thought he heard the bell 20 seconds too soon and ended the round.

47.
George Foreman
Kinshasa
Oct. 30, 1974
KO in 8th

48.
Chuck Wepner
Cleveland
Mar. 24, 1975
KO in 15th

49.
Ron Lyle
Las Vegas
May 16, 1975
KO in 11th

50.
Joe Bugner
Malaysia
June 30, 1975
Decision in 15